TURNING TRIALS INTO TRIUMPHS

MICHELLE CHAVIS   NICHOLE PAGE

SHAVONNA FUTRELL   VENITA ALDERMAN

PATRICIA ALSTON-TAPP   ASHA JONES-WADE

TRACEY BURWELL DESHAZO

VLR BOOKS

TURNING TRIALS INTO TRIUMPHS

.

ACKNOWLEDGMENTS

I thank God for being faithful even when I was not and for the vision to impact the lives of others. I dedicate this accomplishment to my Mother, Yvonne Chavis Ford, whose nurturing and love has given me the strength to persevere and achieve my goals. To my children, LaTicia and Trevon for their unconditional love, encouragement and patience. My mom and children are literally the "Wind Beneath My Wings". To Jocelyn Thompson for always challenging me to be greater. To Angel Jones, Tonya Bullock, Torrie Stanley, Lasheera Lee, Teresa Bobbitt, Twana Bruce, Toya Mayes, Keshia Muhammad. To my Spiritual mothers Patricia Tapp and June Moore, thank you for covering, believing in, and always pushing me – *Michelle Chavis*

First and foremost, I will like to thank God for not allowing me to slip through his fingers but carried me through this journey giving me peace and sanity. My parents for their unconditional love, prayers, inspirations, and allowing me to shed my tears. To my siblings, close cousins, special friends, and Victorious Ladies Reading Book Club for their fellowship, encouragement, and laughter. – *Nichole Page*

First I would like to thank god for giving me the strength to make it through this story. I would like to thank my husband, Robert for helping me relive this story so I could write it, my son Dominique for giving me the ok and encouragement to keep going. JaQuan and Taavonna for their hugs when I was going through the emotional parts. VLR President Michelle Chavis for her vision on this book and my VLR sisters for their encouragement and prayers. Lachelle Weaver for encouraging me. Marion McNair for always being there when I need her the most. – *Shavonna Futrell*

I want to thank my Mom for her unconditional love, my brother for always having my back and my children for being the reason I choose to stay strong. I wish my Dad was still here so he could see my smiles and hear my laughter, thank you Daddy for loving me even when I acted unlovable. I want to thank everyone I have come in contact with because you all have shaped me into the woman I am today. The good, bad and/or indifference. I am thankful for it. – *Venita Alderman*

I would like to thank my family for their support. My mother, Barbara Jones, my brothers, PT and Omar Jones and my kids Sadiq, Jabari, Kareem and Karimah. In memory of my father, Paul Thomas Jones, Jr and my Nana, Marion Gertrude Burt who helped mold me along my journey to perfection. My book club for having this anthology. A special thank you to my cousin and President of VLR, Michelle Chavis, for pushing me outside of my box, which allowed me to experience a whole new world. My VLR sisters are the sisters I have been waiting for my whole life. Thank you and

I am honored to be on this journey with you all. I thank God for this opportunity because I know that all of this is because of him. – *Asha Jones Wade*

I give thanks to my heavenly Father for His unconditional love for me, letting me know I was worth saving. I thank my husband James for his patience & encouraging me to just write. To my beautiful daughter Tracey & granddaughter Tasia for their time and doing my typing with positive feedback. To all my VLR daughters for allowing me to be a part of a book club that is so much more. – *Patricia Alston-Tapp*

First and foremost, I would like to thank God for creating me to be the mother of the Perfect Daughter. My husband for his love, prayers, and words of encouragement. To the ladies of Victorious Ladies Reading Book Club (VLR) for believing that I could tell my story and not letting me give up. Lastly, I would like to give a special thanks to my daughter, Tasia, for being that beacon of light and encouraging me to write her story from my perspective…I love her to infinity and beyond! – *Tracey Burwell-DeShazo*

SPECIAL ACKNOWLEDGMENTS

FOR JACQUELIN THOMAS

Michelle Chavis

To my Writing Coach, Jacquelin Thomas, for sacrificing her time and sharing wisdom to make sure this vision came into fruition.

Nichole Page

I would love to give a special thanks to you, Jacquelin Thomas, for not only being a great mentor but allowing God to use you as our Philosopher by giving us the knowledge and tools to succeed through our writing journey…thank you and bless you so much.

Shavonna Futrell

I would like to thank Jacquelin Thomas for all of her time and encouragement with helping me write this story so I could encourage someone else. Thank you for telling me to breathe and just write and it is ok to do it wrong.

Venita Alderman

I want to thank Jacquelin for sowing into our group.

When we talk about the tree, she has truly been good soil to keep the tree nourished and growing. Jacquelin has sacrificed her time, experience, and her heart into all of us. She is genuine in her love for writing and helping others reach their potential and for that I will always be grateful.

Asha Karimah Jones-Wade

A special thank you to Jacquelin Thomas. I cannot believe that one of my favorite authors helped me make the dream of becoming a published author come true. Thank you so much for your support, guidance and dedication to us and helping our vision come to fruition. Much love and respect to you.

Patricia Alston-Tapp

I want to thank Author Jacquelin Thomas for working diligently with me and being a great encourager

Tracey Burwell DeShazo

Thank you, Jacquelin Thomas for being my mentor, sharing her knowledge, and guiding me every step of the way.

INTRODUCTION

Who are the ladies of VLR? We are mothers, sisters, daughters, wives and friends. We are readers, entrepreneurs and writers. By definition victorious means triumphant, successful or winning. Victorious Ladies Reading Book club is a sisterhood of women that have come together because of our love for books. Seven of us have decided to write a book and share our journey from adversity to victory. The Bible declares that, "We shall be like a tree planted by the rivers of water, that brings forth its fruit in its season, whose leaf also shall not wither; and whatever we do shall prosper."

As you read our stories, meditate on the following scripture: "And the seeds that fell on the good soil represent honest, good-hearted people who hear God's word, cling to it, and patiently produce a huge harvest." Luke 8:15 NLT.

Psalms 1:3 (paraphrased) Green, like the leaves on the branches, symbolizes nature, fertility, and life. It also represents balance, learning, growth and harmony. Our image of the willow tree, on our book cover relates to the strength, stability and structure of the trunk, standing firm on the

Word of God, and withstanding the greatest of challenges that each of us express in our stories.

"For I know the plans I have for you," declares the LORD, "plans to prosper you and not to harm you, plans to give you hope and a future."
Jeremiah 29:11 NIV

"Being confident of this very thing, that He (God) who has begun a good work in you will complete it until the day of Jesus Christ;"
Philippians 1:6 NKJV

No matter what we go through, know that we serve a God that always cause us to triumph. Trust God when you can't trace God and watch Him turn your trial into a triumph.

DADDY'S GIRL

VENITA ALDERMAN

There are so many statistics on how girls grow up in a home without their biological father, how they wed as teenagers, become mothers as teenagers and some go as far at to commit suicide because of the problems they may have faced in fatherless homes.

I didn't grow up in a home with my biological father, but I had the best FATHER that a young girl could ask for. I was a "Daddy's Girl" and I was still broken because of that missing piece *my biological father*.

I was broken but not shattered, and this story will show you it is possible to go from bitter to better.

~ J A M E S O N ~

Qmy life was forever changed one Saturday in
March 2004—the day I knew the world had
to be coming to an end. Especially my world. My insides felt
like something was shredding it to pieces—like when you
watch a food processor chop up vegetables.

I couldn't breathe.

My weak attempts to cough were in vain because I was
choking on the air trying to escape my throat. I felt like I was
drowning in air.

As I lay on my Dad's chilled to the bone body, I tried to
understand why the man I had loved since I was two years
old, was gone and a part of me died with him at that very
moment. Thankfully, I wasn't there alone. His best friend,
Jake stood on the other side of the bed, tears streaming down
his face.

Medical staff flooded the room, turning off machines and
checking on my dad. A nurse informed us that the doctor
would be there shortly.

Jake tried to shake me out of my shock by saying, "You
need to call your mother and brother. They should be here."

He was right. I needed to tell them about Dad. They left the hospital earlier that afternoon, in route to my house to drop off McDonalds to my kids. During my Dad's stay at the hospital, I spent most of my time there, so everyone took shifts in helping with my children. I was appreciative of the support because I really needed to be there for my dad. He needed me and I was not going to abandon him.

Despite him being in the hospital, nothing could've prepared me for what was to come.

* * *

ON FEBRUARY 20TH, my brother rang my phone a few times that morning. At the time, I was headed toward Linwood Middle School, so I didn't answer until I arrived to the school and the kids began getting off the bus. I was one of the drivers at the time.

"What?" I exclaimed. "You know I'm still on my run."

"Something is wrong with Daddy, they taking him to the hospital." He said.

"What do you mean something is wrong with him? What happened?"

"I don't' know, he couldn't breathe or something, I think he was having a heart attack."

"Boy, he is not having a heart attack, now where are they taking him?" I screeched.

"Robert Wood Hospital."

"Call Mommy. I'm on my way, I'll be there in twenty minutes." I was shouting by now, mostly out of fear.

"Alright," He said.

The call ended.

I didn't know how I expected to get there in twenty minutes, but I had to figure something out. I looked to my right and in the first seat sitting with her baby doll sat my four-year-old, youngest daughter, Jordan. I would normally drop her off to preschool in New Brunswick right after my run so when I dropped the bus back off to the garage in South Brunswick; I could get right on the highway and head to Edison to Middlesex County College; where I was enrolled at the time getting my Associates degree in Education.

I pulled out of the school's lot and took the quickest way to Route 1, I decided to take the bus back and then drop Jordan off at school since the hospital was in New Brunswick too. When I got to the hospital I started feeling uneasy. I have never been a huge fan of the hospital and with the emergency room being so chaotic.

I was already on edge, and going through a range of emotions. I was scared, angry, scared... angry... worried... angry because I couldn't get there fast enough.

I tried not to worry because I figured he had indigestion or heart burn, but after the doctor checked him out, we found that he had actually had a stroke. And he never survived.

My Dad was a hard worker and a good man, I know most people say that about their parents but he was. He worked construction for over twenty-five years and he provided for our family. He didn't have to take care of me, but he did. I have recollections of him from the age of two or three. I remembered the brown car he used to drive; It was a Lincoln Mark V. I could recall the leather bomber jackets he would wear with the ragged wool hat and the old spice cologne he would wear. I still have the Keith Sweat cassette tapes he loved to play.

I was his little girl.

Even when he and my Mom split up, he still provided for me, not just financially, but emotionally, spiritually and mentally. Never once did I question if I was loved by him; he showed it daily.

He was like a superhero to his grandkids, my kids. He came by every weekend to bring the kids fruit and me a random plant that he would have to take back the following week because I hadn't watered it and they'd start to wilt.

I called on my Dad for everything; if something was broken in the house... Daddy come fix it. If the car was acting up... Daddy come fix it. If I was short on cash, Daddy... and I ran out of gas on more than a few occasions and who did I call, yup my Dad. Kids needed something, Daddy... or I'd just let them pick up the phone and Grandpa him down... I had a man, but I preferred my Dad to do whatever I needed done. I'd call him daily just to see what he was doing, and he'd be watching TV shaking his glass, I would hear the ice cubes hitting each other. I could picture him swirling his glass around to make sure all the liquid had a nice chill to it. He may not have been my biological father, but he was the best dad any girl could hope for—he was a great man and I loved him dearly.

The day I received that phone call from my brother—I had no idea it would lead me to a place of grief, a place of hurt... a place of unimaginable loss.

I ended up graduating that December instead of May because I had taken a semester off during my father's illness. I had already missed two weeks of school and knew I wouldn't be able to focus on my school work, during the time he was in the hospital. I didn't' even bother to attend my graduation because my Dad wasn't there. It wasn't the same without him.

My Dad also wasn't able to walk me down the aisle. I didn't get to do the Daddy and Daughter dance. But Jake was there, and that made me feel like my Dad was present in spirit. He told me after the ceremony and reception was over that my Dad was there. We cremated my Dad and split the ashes, I wanted Jake to have some to spread across the ocean where they fished, and he kept a little and had it in a small satin bag in his jacket pocket.

1 Corinthians 13 tells us: *"Though I speak with the tongues of men and of angels, but have not love, I have become sounding brass or a clanging cymbal. ² And though I have the gift of prophecy, and understand all mysteries and all knowledge, and though I have all faith, so that I could remove mountains, but have not love, I am nothing. ³ And though I bestow all my goods to feed the poor, and though I give my body to be burned, but have not love, it profits me nothing. ⁴ Love suffers long and is kind; love does not envy; love does not parade itself, is not puffed up; ⁵ does not behave rudely, does not seek its own, is not provoked, thinks no evil; ⁶ does not rejoice in iniquity, but rejoices in the truth; ⁷ bears all things, believes all things, hopes all things, endures all things. ⁸ Love never fails. But whether there are prophecies, they will fail; whether there are tongues, they will cease; whether there is knowledge, it will vanish away. ⁹ For we know in part and we prophesy in part. ¹⁰ But when that which is perfect has come, then that which is in part will be done away. ¹¹ When I was a child, I spoke as a child, I understood as a child, I thought as a child; but when I became a man, I put away childish things. ¹² For now we see in a mirror, dimly, but then face to face. Now I know in part, but then I shall know just as I also am known. ¹³ And now abide faith, hope, love, these three; but the greatest of these is love."*

My dad—my superhero was gone, leaving me alone with my memories.

~ISAAC~

*N*ow I had Isaac, but instead of being a superman to me—he was more of the boogie man.

My mom never said anything about him to me, good or bad. All my feelings are my own, from my personal experiences with him.

I have no recollection of spending time with Isaac as a child. I do remember the few times he called and promised me a present. He had me waiting on the mailman, like most kids waited on the ice cream truck to come when they heard the song and bell ringing from two blocks away. Isaac called once in October and told me he is sorry he missed my birthday.

I was born in November.

Then a few years later called in December and said he knows he got it right this time, thinking he was calling ahead, and it was already over. That's how the conversations went. I don't remember being asked about my day, how I did in school or any of my interest. I just heard unkempt promises; so I associate him with lies.

John 8:44 tells us: *"You are of your father the devil, and the desires of your father you want to do. He was a murderer from the beginning, and does not stand in the truth, because there is no truth in him. When he speaks a lie, he speaks from his own resources, for he is a liar and the father of it."*

Satan is often referenced as the father of lies, but my biological father could probably challenge him for the title. His conversations were always filled with half-truths, whole lies... anything but what it really was.

I was good, despite grieving for my dad. I wasn't looking for a replacement father. I was fine.

Even if I were, I never would've called on Isaac. He had never been on my radar and this hadn't changed with losing my dad.

~ATTEMPTS~

$\mathcal{T}$hree weeks after my Dad died, imagine my shock when Isaac called my cell phone. I was sitting outside Little Caesars waiting on my kids Pizza. I rewarded them with Pizza on Friday's as a treat for having a good week.

When the phone rang, I didn't recognize the number, but I had been getting calls from various people just checking in on me so I answered, "Hello."

"Vivian?"

"Yes, who is this?"

"How are you doing?"

"Fine, who is this?" I asked again.

"Your father."

My entire body tensed up as I looked at my phone.

"Hello, Vivian are you there?"

My brain was still trying to process what my ears just heard. I had a jerk on my phone pretending to be my Dad and I was furious. I had just buried him and didn't appreciate anyone playing on my phone like this. "Listen, my father is dead. Don't call this phone again!" I was just getting started on the curse out I was going to give that caller, when he announced, "Vivian, this is Isaac."

Time seemed like it stood still for a brief moment.

This did nothing to improve my mood. He was not someone I was interested in talking to at any point in my life. "Don't you EVER call my phone and introduce yourself as my father, my father just died!" I yelled.

"I heard about it, I'm sorry to hear that. Jameson was a really good guy." He stated.

"I know. *Goodbye.*" I hung up the phone.

Although I tried to keep my tears from falling—they won the battle and I cried.

The next time I heard from Isaac was a few months later.

He showed up on my doorstep.

I don't think I'll ever find out how he knew where I lived this time; I actually had five kids by then, so you can do the math with how many years had passed.

He knocked on my door and my kids ran to the door, they looked out the window and yelled to me that there was a man at the door and they didn't know who he was.

I went to the door and he was standing there. I didn't want to upset my kids by instantly yelling at him, because Lord knows I wanted to cuss him from his head to his toe. Instead, I asked in the softest voice I could muster up, "What are you doing here?"

He asked me to introduce him to my children and I did. I told them he was a stranger and asked them what they were supposed to do when a stranger tried to talk to them.

They started yelling as loud as they could while pointing to him.

"Stranger danger."

After a good thirty seconds of all that yelling, I told them to go back to playing. I stepped outside and shut the door behind me.

We stayed outside for no more than five minutes, because that was how much of my time I was willing to let him waste.

Deep down, I felt like I was betraying my Dad by entertaining Isaac for that long.

He had a camera and tried to snap pictures of me and asked if he could take pictures of my children, the answer was no and after I let him talk about himself and a traumatic event he experienced I went back in the house. I don't think I will ever understand how or why he thought anything pertaining to him or his life meant anything to me.

I should have screamed *"stranger danger"* along with my kids because I didn't know him either. See, I was still trying to hold it together for my family, smiling and functioning during the day but scared to go to sleep at night because I wasn't ready to experience seeing my Dad in my dreams.

* * *

ISAAC CALLED AGAIN.

I was more than irritated with his attempts to build a relationship with me. We had already had several arguments on the phone, which were so intense that my husband would make me hang up the phone.

Isaac often asked off the wall questions and made sarcastic statements whenever we talked. I didn't like to be questioned especially by someone who I felt didn't add any value to any part of my life. It seemed like he would call every four or five years; and the particular year he called, he would call twice.

JEREMIAH 10:19 SAYS: *"Woe is me for my hurt! My wound is severe. But I say, truly this is an infirmity, And I must bear it."*

~PISSED OFF~

The second call of that year I received from Isaac infuriated me because, he put a little girl on the phone name whose name was Vivianna. He introduced her as his daughter.

I realized he was not only a liar but a manipulator as well. It wasn't because he had a daughter, but because he named her something so close to my name. I felt like he did it in effort to have a do over with fathering a daughter. I wanted to speak to the mother and ask her why would she even allow such shenanigans, but I chose to remain quiet and shake yet this other open hand slap I felt I received. I was stunned.

Vivianna was happy to talk to me, happy to have a big sister. This girl was younger than my youngest child. So I had to talk to her as if she was one of my children, I asked her how she liked school, her favorite color, if she played sports and what she wanted to be when she grew up. After about ten minutes it was time for me to end the call, because I was running out of things to ask her. I told her she could call me anytime she wanted and before I could say goodbye, she told me Dad wanted to speak with me... with that last statement I hung up the phone. If only I could really speak to my Dad again, but I couldn't. All I had were his ashes, pictures and my memories...

I got another call and he asked if he could tell me a story; I thought, let me humor this approach.

"Don't you think I'm too old for stories?" I asked.

"Can you just hear me out, I want to explain things," Isaac said.

"You missed how many decades? Over four, so guess how many stories I've heard in my lifetime already?" I responded sarcastically.

"Can you hear one more?" He pleaded.

"I got a couple of minutes then I have to go," I snapped.

"Vivian, first I want to tell you that I love you very much and not a day goes by that I don't think about you," He said.

I quickly interrupted by blurting, "I already don't like this story."

"Let me finish," he pleaded, "I wanted to be a family, but your Mom wanted to go out with this guy name Fred with a Red Thunderbird. I tried, but she wanted him. And then when she met Jameson, he was a good guy so I knew you would be okay."

"So you trying to blame my Mom for leaving you as to why you didn't do your part in raising me? Is that what just came out your mouth? My Dad was a good guy, so you thought it was okay to abandon me? You are something else. Well, thank you for the best thing you could have ever done."

"I don't understand," He stated.

"Your absence was the best thing you did for me, because I got the best Dad, and it wasn't you," I snapped.

"Do you read the bible?" He asked.

"What?" *He caught me off guard by that question.* "Of course

I do!" I screamed through the phone, as I looked over on my nightstand at my Bible.

"Well it says you should honor your mother and father."

I think I lost all the religious teaching I had ever learned and heard.

I muttered a string of curses. "I did honor my parents, and you aren't in that particular group." *By now, I have grabbed my Bible, ready to hit him scripture per scripture about how he needed to take care of his responsibility.* "You're a sorry excuse for a man." I hung up the phone.

"I don't know why you take his calls, if all it does is get you upset," Lance said.

I looked up at him as he stood in the doorway of our bedroom. "I don't know either, but what I do know is this crap ends today with him."

I called my Mom after Isaac tried to blame her for not being there.

"Ma," I yelled through the receiver.

"What's wrong?" She said.

"Let me tell you what Isaac had the nerve to say."

"What?" She asked.

"Who is Freddy?" I questioned.

"I don't know. Where is he from?"

"Your old *boyfriend*." I laughed. Just hearing my mother's voice was a calming mechanism.

"What in the world are you talking about?" She chuckled.

"Isaac said that he wanted to be a family with you but you wanted Freddy with the Red Thunderbird."

Now she was laughing. "Red Thunderbird?"

"Yup, that's what he said."

"Well, you are talking how many years ago. I don't remember no mess like that," she said.

"That's my point; he is telling me this mess like it just happened yesterday and I had a choice in the matter."

"Oh boy," she responded.

"Yes, oh boy is right. You traumatized him in high school with Red Thunderbird boy and he's traumatizing me for life." I laughed.

"I wonder who he talking about though." She said.

"Why you want to go look for Freddy, the home wrecker?" I laughed.

"No silly, but anyway and other than that, how was your day?" She asked.

And just like that, I was diffused and we talked about other things until I had to go tend to my family.

After that, I decided I needed to work on why I was still so angry with him. I stopped answering calls that didn't have a name associated with it on my caller ID.

Vivianna called and left messages and I would return her calls. We talked for a few minutes and I would disconnect the call whenever she mentioned that her father wanted to talk to me.

PHILIPPIANS 4:6-7: *"Do not be anxious about anything, but in every situation, by prayer and petition, with thanksgiving, present your requests to God. And the peace of God, which transcends all understanding, will guard your hearts and your minds in Christ Jesus."*

~MY LETTER~

J wrote him a letter once I found myself in a better place; spiritually, mentally and emotionally to deal with him. I had to first learn to just forgive him. It was the past and I survived and turned out okay. I realized all I ever wanted was an apology, and it was clear I would never get it because he continued to have an excuse or place blame on others for his absenteeism.

Isaac,

I am not angry with you anymore and I still don't want anything to do with you. All I needed was an apology and I understand that's something you will not be able to give and it's okay. All I ask is that you allow me to have a relationship with Vivianna without you getting involved.

Vivian

As I sealed the envelope, relief washed over me. It was finished. I said all that I felt was necessary to say and now I was done. I was proud of myself for not writing a note filled with profanity, accusations and such. We would never have a real father-daughter relationship and I was okay with this.

MATTHEW 11:29-30: *"Take my yoke upon you and learn from me, for I am gentle and humble in heart, and you will find rest for your souls. For my yoke is easy and my burden is light."*

~RESOLUTION~

$\mathcal{I}$ had always wondered why my father didn't love me enough to take care of me; why he had other children and took care of them. However, he simply walked away from a two-year-old little girl. I have always questioned this as a child and even into my adult years. I've always felt a little unwanted and insecure. It was not until I began self-evaluating myself through Isaac's actions.

It used to get on my nerves when people would say, God does everything for a reason... Really? I used to think... But it's a little deeper than that. See, God knew Isaac had nothing to give me– Jameson did. And that's why he was there.

I also had to learn that all the strength and my resilience comes from God, my Heavenly Father.

Jameson gave me everything he had, which was unconditional love. He continuously pumped positive encouragement into me–we just never knew there was a small leak (Isaac) that had no plug. That leak has since been plugged, but the journey wasn't easy.

I made it.

I'm standing strong, happy, and accomplished. I was

broken but not shattered. The pieces have been put back together.

MARK 11:25: *"And whenever you stand praying, if you have anything against anyone, forgive him, that your Father in heaven may also forgive you your trespasses."*

~VICTORY~

I hope after reading this story you are able to find peace within a broken situation. Sometimes you may feel that all you need is an apology, but there are some people who can't or won't give you that. Some of these individuals may feel that their actions were justifiable. Sometimes it is pride and the shame of admitting a wrong—there are many reasons why people do what they do. However, their actions are not your concern.

This is when you have to dig deep within yourself and acknowledge all the emotions (abandonment, grief, hurt, lost, anger, etc.) you may feel. The first step to healing is to recognize that these are very real emotions. Second, you have to choose to either be bitter or better. I chose to make be a better person in spite of what Isaac did or didn't do for me. I refused to allow his treatment of me to define the woman I would become. Instead, his mistakes made me a better parent.

Do whatever it takes to heal, to forgive and finally move forward. Self-evaluation and forgiveness makes a huge difference in moving forward with your life. There is no time limit in the healing, just continue to strive for peace within yourself.

JEREMIAH 29:11: *"For I know the plans I have for you," declares the Lord, "plans to prosper you and not to harm you, plans to give you hope and a future."*

VENITA ALDERMAN SADLER is originally from New Jersey but currently lives in North Carolina with her family. Venita holds degrees in Education, Business Management and is currently pursuing a Masters in Accounting. Venita is an entrepreneur (4-5 Essentials) and currently working on a trilogy titled "A Family of Secrets." Venita is a National Best Selling co-author of The Ex-Chronicles, where her short story "Online Secrets" is featured. Stay in touch at: www.VenitaAldermanSadler.com and/or on Amazon, Goodreads, Facebook and Instagram (Venita Alderman Sadler) and on Twitter (VenitaASadler).

FINDING SEVEN: PERFECTING MY IMPERFECTIONS

ASHA JONES-WADE

No one picks who their parents are, but everyone has them. No matter what capacity they have in your life, their absence and presence affects you, your views and ways in life. It is so ironic that even if you never know your father or never have had a relationship with him, his transgressions can have a major impact on your life. His genes make up half of yours and even if you have never seen him before he has an effect on your life.

I can sympathize with people who do not have a relationship with their mother and/or father but I cannot empathize. I know that there are a lot of people walking around that have been greatly affected by the lack of paternal or maternal love. I have a close relationship with both of my parents and cannot imagine the effect that their absence would have on my life.

My mother is someone who mourns the absence of her biological father. I didn't know who he was until I was in high school. I grew up with a grandfather (my grandmother's husband) for the first seven years of my life. My grandfather passed away when I was seven years old. To me, that was my maternal grandfather. Eight years later, my mother dropped a bomb on me one Sunday after church that the beloved deacon who used to shake my hand after church was her biological father. I had so many questions. I was shocked. My mother is such an awesome person. Why wasn't he a part of her life? How can you walk away from someone who has half of your DNA?

The more I looked at Deacon Deadbeat, the more I saw how much my mother looked like him. Maybe even more than his other kids. How can he look at us and not want a relationship with us either? I remember the day I went to my biological grandfather's funeral and I didn't shed one tear. I have been to funerals of people I barely knew and cried, but I could not bring myself to cry for the loss of a man that did not acknowledge my mother or us in his life. Especially since he took care of a daughter that is not biologically his. I tried not to be sitting up in church feeling this way. Listening to his "daughter" talk about daddy this, and daddy that–it made me want to throw up. My mother did not come to the funeral and I can understand why. I just wonder how she felt. She had already lost her father once in that he was not a part of her life. She is not the type of person to wish for malicious things to happen to anyone no matter how much hurt and pain they may have caused.

I am somewhat obsessed with numbers. I think that numbers are significant to everything that we do in life. I think that everyone has numbers that are significant to them and their life. I think that my numbers are 3,4 and 7. The number seven is the number of completion.

Seven days in the week.

Seven deadly sins.

Seven colors in the rainbow.

Seven is a significant number in society and in my life. There are many ways you can get to seven (7+0), (6+1), (5+2). I think that my way to seven is (3+4).

Everyone strives for perfection. To live in the perfect house. To drive the perfect car. To be the perfect size. I used to want everything to be perfect and if it wasn't, then I felt some type of way. I also tried to be everything to everyone, while neglecting myself. I remember one Sunday at church we had Women's Day. The speaker spoke about breaking the Superwoman complex. I was listening to the speaker and realized that she was talking about me. I realized that I would put too many "irons to the fire" and take on too much.

I had to learn that there was no shame in asking for help, which is difficult for me. In this season of my life I am striving to be a Proverbs 31 type of woman. I am also making myself more open to new opportunities.

I am one of three children. I have three boys and a girl. My fourth child was born on 4/4/12 (12 is 3x4). Numbers are constantly ringing in my head.

I was born in the third month of the year at 3:49 pm. I found out I was pregnant with my oldest child on 4/7/98 and he was born 10/7/98. I was married 4/21/2001 (7x3=21). I got the keys to my first house on the first day of July (7/1). In 2016, which I call the year of 7, I started working at the VA medical center in Durham in July, which is the seventh month.

When it comes to numbers, my odd birthdays have been bittersweet and the even years rough.

However, despite the roads I've had to travel in my life— I've learned a lot about myself in the process.

CHAPTER 2

*I*n 2006, (my 27th birthday) my husband Tony asked me for a divorce.

I felt like someone had kicked me in the gut. Once the shock wore off, I began to feel like a failure because my marriage hadn't worked out.

It was an awful feeling to find that the person you vowed to spend the rest of your life with—wanted out. Like any other marriage, we had our share of problems, but perhaps we could've tried harder to make the relationship work.

The women in my family seem to end up single and I felt I had inherited this same curse—destined to be alone for the rest of my life. My nana was a widow and never remarried. My mother is single currently and has been since she and my father divorced almost thirty years ago. My aunt is also single.

Since my divorce, I haven't really been in a relationship and to be honest—I'm not really sure why. I often wonder if it's because I'm afraid to give so much of myself to someone else only to have them forsake me ten years down the road?

But as much as I'm afraid to love and be heartbroken, I am more afraid that I will die a lonely spinster.

There is a small part of me that believes I can't move on because of unresolved feelings that I have toward my ex-husband. I am trying my best to successfully co-parent our four children with him, so I really don't want to complicate our relationship.

Loneliness can sometimes make you rush out and settle for the first man to garner your attention. This was not the path I wanted to take. The ending of my marriage was very painful for me and so I am extremely protective of my heart.

I decided the best decision for me is to pray and wait on the Lord to handle this area of my life. I believe that if I stay faithful and the closer my relationship is with GOD; He will bring the man He has chosen to be my life's mate. I am content in my singleness and am in no rush to run out and run smack into Mr. Dead Wrong.

In the meantime, I spend my time focusing on my children and being the best mother possible.

*I*n 2010 (my 31st birthday), I lost my apartment. I was living in Maryland at the time. This was a terrible time for me. I was homeless for three months.

I found that people can be a bit judgmental when it comes to homelessness. Not everyone living on the streets are crazy, substance abusers, or bums. There are good people who found themselves in a situation where they could not keep their homes. The reality is that homelessness is a hard situation without a lot of great solutions, and the consequences of homelessness for anyone can be dismal. When a whole family is homeless, it carries with it the possibility that the children could be taken into state custody. As you can imagine, this was a very scary time for me. My sons and I made our home in a hotel, which was very costly. At this rate, it was impossible to save money. I really didn't see a way out of my circumstances.

However, I found out that the Lord is faithful and He provided refuge for me when I had nowhere to go. A coworker offered me a place to stay and I am forever grateful to her.

I eventually made the decision to move back home, so I packed up my family and moved them to North Carolina. Looking back, it was the best decision for my us. There are times when you have to go home and regroup.

Since coming home, we have been able to thrive and get back on our feet. New lessons learned, I moved on, ready for the next phase of experiences.

The important thing about life is that there is so much to learn—many ways to grow. I look forward to each year with renewed hope for the future.

The next few years weren't that bad for me. My family and I continued to thrive and my faith continued to mature. There was still more to learn.

*I*n 2014 (my 35th birthday), my father had a stroke and passed away. In the very same week, one of my classmates was murdered by his wife. Over the course of the next few years, I had to learn a lot about loss.

In 2016, my beloved grandmother passed away three days before my 37th birthday. Her funeral was on my birthday. I also lost two cousins this year.

Losing my father and my grandmother placed apprehension in me about losing my mother. I know that one day I will have to live life without her, but I have to confess that the thought terrifies me. My mother is my emergency contact. Who else can I depend on in case of emergency? She is the only person I trust others to call if I can't make decisions for myself.

I am afraid of being alone. However, this is a part of my maturity. I am working to build and expand my social network. I've built a wonderful inner circle and am slowly increasing my emergency contact list.

This year hasn't been all bad.

My oldest son graduated from high school and he has

started college. I am graduating from college. KJ, my twin brother finished up his high school requirements and is getting his high school diploma. He will then take classes to get a degree to work as a fire inspector. My oldest brother, who has hydrocephalus and was told that he would not live to be twenty, turned forty this year and is in good health.

This year, I set seven (7) goals for myself on my 37th birthday.

My first goal is to complete my bachelor's degree this year. A long term goal is to go to law school. My second goal is to attend church more and become more active in the church. After my father passed away, it became very hard for me to go to church. I'm not sure why, maybe it was because I was angry over losing my father, but I'm working on my relationship with the Lord. My third goal is to become a published author. My fourth goal is to lose these last fifteen pounds and change to a healthier lifestyle. All of my immediate family members have hypertension—I don't want it and I intend to do whatever I need to do to keep it this way. My fifth goal is to continue to try new things and expand my talents. Last year, I bought a professional camera and this year, I bought a sewing machine and a serger. I love taking pictures like my father did so I'm working to expand my photography skills. I also want to do more sewing. My desire is to make a quilt like the ones my grandmother and great grandmother uses to make. My sixth goal is to take a annual trip with my kids to places we've never been before, and my seventh goal is to become more organized. It is a process and I'm working on it daily.

I think of life and words like good (which is 4 letters) and bad (which is 3 letters) equals seven. Glad and mad, live and die these words are opposites of each other and they describe life and they equal up to seven letters. Life is all about finding your seven. It won't be easy all the time, but sometimes you need to go through certain situations to make you stronger. You have to take the good with the bad to fulfill your destiny (which is a 7 letter word).

I'm perfect in my imperfections, happy in my pain, strong in my weaknesses and beautiful in my own way cause I'm me. I am learning daily that my perfect is specific to me and everything I do and every choice that I make is taking me one step closer to finding my "Seven."

ASHA JONES WADE is a native of North Carolina. She is a pharmacy technician by trade. She is currently attending Walden University and working towards a degree in Political Science and Public Administration with a concentration in Law and Legal Studies. Asha has three sons and one daughter. She loves to shop, read and spend time with her family. Asha loves the Lord and is very involved with the church and community. One of her favorite scriptures is: 1 Corinthians 2:9 "Eyes have not seen, nor ears heard, nor have entered into the heart of man; the things which God has prepared for those who love Him." You can contact Asha at: ashakwade@gmail.com.

LEADING WITH A LIMP

SHAVONNA FUTRELL

He who limps is still walking.

We may limp along but we are still going forward! Never underestimate God's presence based on your predicament. God will use the very thing that the enemy meant for your bad and work it together for your good.

The good news is that whenever someone finds him or herself off the path of God, reconciling with Him is an instant thing. God will never withhold His forgiveness from us. Although we limp, we are still walking.

Thank you for your

support S. Futrell

CHAPTER 1

Your word is a lamp to my feet and a light to
my path.

Psalms119:105 NKJV

"om, are you going to church today?" My son
Devon asked.

"I had not planned on it," I responded. "Why?"

"I really want to go and the church bus has already come."

"Okay, go get dressed and we will go." If my child was that eager to go to church, I was definitely going to take him.

We arrived just in time for the eleven o'clock service.

I can't really remember what the message was that Sunday, but the pastor's words touched my son so much that when he asked. "Is there anyone here that doesn't know Jesus but want to get to know him—please come down to the altar."

My heart grew full as I watched my son walk down to the front. This was the greatest feeling I had experienced in a long time, witnessing my 12-year-old give his life to the Lord.

There are really no words to explain my joy over this movement of God. There is a certain peace that comes with knowing that your child has a heart for the Lord and is willing to seek out a relationship with Him.

The thought crossed my mind of what I would've missed out on if I had not come to church, but more than that—I was so proud of my son.

Nothing could overshadow the beautiful blessing of my son entering into a personal relationship with Christ. It never occurred to me during this joyous moment that these are the times when Satan seeks to steal, kill and destroy. I never considered that my son would soon become a target of the enemy.

CHAPTER 2

 y son and I started going to this church every Sunday and became very involved, participating in events and learning more about our Heavenly Father.

Three months passed and our youth pastor announced that my son had confided in him that God had called him to preach.

Wow.

It was a wonderful announcement and it thrilled me to no end, but there was also a small measure of fear. I knew Satan was going to attack my son. He certainly didn't want another person walking around spreading God's word. I prayed for the Lord to cover him.

My family and I continued our work with the church. I joined the children's ministry, women's ministry, and helped with anything that needed to be done.

This experience had brought my son and I even closer, so we did everything together. He was a part of the children's ministry; he went out with the men of the church, witnessing to people and inviting them to attend church.

I could see that God was really working in our lives. We were growing in the knowledge of the Word of God. Our faith was maturing. God was so good to us.

My son was truly on fire for God and I enjoyed watching him walk in his calling. It was truly a blessing to behold and I was so thankful. I felt peace in knowing that God had His hand on my baby and would protect him. Pastor B had a great effect on my son and had become his mentor.

It was a wonderful time in our lives.

CHAPTER 3

Two years later, Pastor B came to talk to us about starting a school at the church. He wanted my husband and I to take our kids out of public school and enroll them into the new school.

We prayed on this decision, asking God to lead us in the right direction for our family since the tuition and school fees were not exactly within our budget at the time.

Although my husband and I hadn't made a decision, we went to the meeting regarding the school to obtain more information. While there, we found that we weren't really comfortable with some of the rules and procedures.

However, shortly after the meeting, Pastor B announced that God wanted his family to move back to New York and start a church there. They would be leaving.

My son was very hurt by the news.

Pastor B and his family left right before the end of the school year of my son's eighth grade year. After he left, I noticed that my son began to act out; talking back, being rebellious and totally out of control. One day during an argument with his father, he blurted out he wanted to go live with his biological mother because he did not like our rules.

Although it hurt, my husband responded, "Fine. Call your mama and see if you can stay with her."

His mother agreed to let him live with her.

This was very hard for me. Even though he was not my biological child, he had been in my life since he was five years old.

No one could tell me he was not my son. I begged my husband not to let him go, but he wanted our son to have this experience. His mother had never really been around for much of his life. Nevertheless, we packed his stuff and delivered him to Bertie County to his mother.

We would soon find out that this would be one of the biggest mistakes we've ever made.

*T*hat fall, Devon joined the football team at his new high school in Bertie County, which was also his father's high school Alma mater. My husband had played football there and was hailed a superstar so my son had to live up to the high standards set by his father.

My son called to let us know the date of his first game so that we could attend.

Although he lived with his biological mother now—we would never miss his games. From the time he was six years old—we had never missed one and would not start now.

He was a good athlete and excelled in everything he did. He had a promising future ahead of him.

We were looking forward to seeing him play football.

Days later, we drove up for his game. I was taken aback by the appearance of my sixteen-year-old son. He stood there with an earring in his ear, his hair grown out—a mass of curly hair. He had done all of the things we wouldn't let him do in our home. Devon looked like a different person to me. Even his stance and persona had changed.

I put my personal feelings aside because I was thrilled to

see him. I'd missed him very much. We had a great time and my son made me proud on the football field. He was a true athlete.

Unfortunately, we were not able to make his next game—it was this night that a part of his future changed. Devon broke his ankle and never played again.

While he was at the hospital, I received a call from my mother-in-law. She told me that my son wanted me there when he came out of surgery.

My baby needed me and I was going, but my husband stopped me. He reminded me that our son chose to go live with his mother. It wasn't a punishment. My husband just felt that Devon's mother should be the one there for him during this time. We lived four hours away.

I wanted to be there badly for my son, and I didn't believe that his mother was able to really take care of him. Several months later I would find out that statement was true.

Every day I would talk to Devon and I could tell something wasn't quite right, but he tried to pretend otherwise.

One day, I asked, "Devon, are you ready to come home yet?" I was joking with him, but his response was a sincere one.

He answered, "Yes ma'am. Please ask Daddy if I can come home."

Needless to say, my husband was ecstatic—we both were over the moon that our son would be coming home to live with us.

We decided to wait until fall break to pick him up, so he could be home to celebrate Christmas with us.

In our joy, we purchased him a desktop computer. We had no idea at the time that this was a big mistake.

A couple of months later, I had to pay bills and asked, "Devon, can I use your computer?"

While sitting at his desk, I noticed a blank check and asked, "Where did you get this check?"

"I found it," he replied.

"Well, you need to throw this away."

I watched as he balled it up and threw it away and considered the matter settled. Little did I know this was just the beginning of what would take our family through the greatest storm of our lives.

We would later find out that this was not a one-time situation. There were several instances where he had stolen checks and tried to purchase things. Devon had even stolen a credit card from the mother of one of his friends. He used it to purchase a laptop computer.

I was so embarrassed to have to tell those people who had treated my son like their own, that he had stolen from them. I found out that they suspected he had been stealing from them for a while. He had taken a watch, money, and other jewelry.

Luckily, they were very understanding and did not press charges--especially since we were able to get their money back.

I had hoped my son would've learned his lesson from this experience. He wasn't a bad kid—I knew this. Devon was MY son and I knew the type of person he was. What I didn't know was why he had taken to stealing. I was very angry and upset with my son, he seemed all nonchalant like it was no big deal. His father hollered and cussed while I just sat there and cried my eyes out.

"Why Devon?" I wanted to know. "Why would you go in her purse and take her credit cards? Did you think she wouldn't notice?"

He just sat there staring off into space.

"Have you ever done anything like this before?"

"Yes, when I lived with my mom, there was no food in the house so I stole hot dogs, cans of ravioli, and stuff like that," he told us, his head bowed down.

"Devon, you had no reason to be stealing no food, your grandparents live fifteen minutes away. Your aunt—all your daddy's family live right there and you could have called us. This makes no sense at all," I stated while trying to remain as calm as I could. "I can't believe this."

I threw my hands up in the air; shook my head and stomped off to my room.

Who is this child in my living room? I wondered. I had raised this child since he was five years old. I never would've believed that my son would ever be a thief.

"*H*ello, you have a collect call from Devon, an inmate in the Guilford County Jail. Will you accept the call?"

I began breathing heavily, my mind raced and tears started to roll down my cheek. "Yes I will accept the call," I said, my voice trembling.

"Devon, what in the world are you doing in jail?"

"Mama please come get me," he pleaded. "Me and my friends went out to lunch and the cops pulled us over and said we fit the description of four young men that just broke in someone house and robbed them."

"We will be down there as soon as your father gets home."

I hung up the phone and I started pacing the floor and talking to God. I begged Him to cover and keep my son safe. My heart hurt so bad it felt like someone was repeatedly stabbing me in my chest. I couldn't do anything but cry, I was so distraught. I couldn't breathe—just gasp for air.

I couldn't believe this was happening to my family.

Devon was released in our custody because he was a minor.

On the way home, I did an interrogation of my own. I wanted to know who he was with; why he left school in the first place—I wanted to know if he was in a gang. I worried that he had a whole set of friends we knew nothing about. I had always made it my business to know all of his friends.

This was the first night of many that I would cry myself asleep as I worried about the future of my oldest child.

CHAPTER 7

$\mathcal{W}$hen we went to court, our prayer was that the judge would dismiss the case due to lack of evidence; Devon had good grades, and had a family that supported him and attended church. The judge asked if the parents had anything to add before he made his judgment and I spoke up and said, "I would like for my son to at least have community service to see that the grass is not greener on the other side and that he is a very fortunate and blessed child."

The judge gave him fifty hours of community service.

Later that day, we went to get his community service assignment. He was assigned to Guilford County Recreation and Parks where he would be helping to clean up the parks and cut grass.

Everything seemed to be going great.

He was doing good in school and we felt like everything was great.

The manager at Guilford County Recreation and Parks talked to us about giving Devon a summer job because he worked his community service hours as if he were getting paid.

When Devon would come home each day after working his community service, he would be so excited about his day. He would tell us all that he was able to do and learn about landscaping. He had not been this excited about anything in a long time. This made me feel like what had happened was just a minor mistake, but now we were back on track and going forward.

* * *

"MAY I speak to the parents of Devon Harmon?"

"This is his mother," I replied.

"Hi ma'am, I'm calling from the Greensboro Police Department. I would like to ask your son some questions about an incident. When would be a good time to come talk to you and your husband?"

"What is this pertaining to?" I asked.

A truck was vandalized and your son's ID was found in the truck.

"Okay," I said. "He should be home soon." A wave of apprehension flowed through me.

"Ma'am, do you know a Jason Fox?"

Jason?

"That's my 10-year-old son. What does he have to do with this?"

"We found a lunch box with his name on it inside the truck."

"Well, his older brother was using it to take his lunch in," I told the officer.

"Do you know where your son was on New Year's Eve?"

"He was out with his friend from down the street." I remembered my son calling me that night to say they were going to be late because they were in High Point with his friend's girlfriend.

"Is it okay to come by at six o'clock?"

"Yes. His father will be home by then."

When we hung up, I immediately called my son's friend and inquired where they went that night.

"I'm sorry, Mrs. Fox. I was not in town I was at the beach with my family."

"Okay… thank you, sweetie. Tell your parents I said hello."

I hung up the phone. "Oh Lord! What has this child done now?"

My son comes home and I demand to know where he was that night.

He lies to me, so I ask a second time.

Not satisfied with his answers, I tell him, "The police called here asking questions about that night. They are coming to talk to you, so you need to tell the truth."

His father arrived.

He had barely gotten into the house when the police pulled up.

We sat down in the living room with the officer who I thought was here to interrogate my son as to his where-abouts on the night in question. However, my son was immediately arrested for stealing a truck.

I have to confess that if I had known they were coming to arrest him, I never would've let them come to the house.

The officer told us someone witnessed my son taking a set of keys to a vehicle. He told us that a laptop was missing and they suspected Devon had taken it as well.

I went into lawyer mode and started firing off questions. "If someone saw him take the keys, then why are they just now saying something? What evidence do you have that makes you so sure it was *my* son? Where are you taking him?"

I broke down and cried. I couldn't believe this was happening again.

We went down to the police station.

We were there for four hours before they released him back into our custody. My husband and I were so disappointed... so hurt... there are no words for the pain we felt. We loved Devon fiercely and we knew his potential—I wanted to wring that boy's neck for this recklessness. We searched for reasons why he had chosen this path, but the truth is that our son had no real idea either.

We had never felt such sadness as a family.

* * *

"Jason, where is your brother?" I asked not too long after the incident with the truck.

"I don't know," he responded. "He didn't ride the bus home. Maybe he had to stay after school."

When time has passed to the point that I knew Devon should be home, I began calling his friends, looking for him.

No one had seen or spoken to Devon.

I called his job just in case he had gone directly to work.

I was informed that he had called in. I requested the number he had called from—I was in detective mode. After doing a reverse lookup, I found out the identity and address.

I was stunned. The address was across the street from us.

The telephone rang.

It was Devon's biological mother.

"Did you know Devon was here with me?" She inquired.

I was surprised since she was four hours away from us. "How did he get there?"

"He drove here in his truck."

"Devon doesn't have a truck."

"He told me that the man across the street gave it to him.

He said he was selling drugs for him and this man gave him the truck. I don't believe nothing he tells me so I figured I'd better call you."

My heart broke as I replied, "Don't say anything to him. Just call the police because I'm sure the truck is stolen."

I hung up.

Devon's mother did as we instructed and our son was arrested.

In the meantime, my husband and I composed ourselves and walked across the street to talk to our neighbor. To add to our heartache and embarrassment, we found out that he had broken into the man's house through a back window. It was how he was able to get the keys to the truck.

Our neighbor was very upset. We assured him that we would pay for fuel and impound expenses so that he could recover his truck from Windsor, North Carolina. We paid out two hundred dollars and requested a signed and notarized letter stating that we paid as promised and also fixed his broken window.

Devon was transported back to Guilford County to await trial. We could've bailed him out, but at this point, we were so frustrated and tired of it all, that my husband and I decided to let him sit in jail—at least, we would know where he was.

One day, Devon's lawyer called and told me they had a program that take school kids out of jail and back in school so that they can continue their education. I was so happy about this because I did not want my son in jail. The lawyer told me that Devon should be ready to go in about an hour. He stated that our son had to stay out of trouble or they would put him back in jail.

I told my boss what was going on and left to pick up my son. God had given my son favor and I hoped Devon would appreciate a second chance to have a life outside of the prison system.

Instead of rejoicing with him, I made a comment that I regret to this day. I asked him, "Are you trying to make this place your permanent residence?"

He just looked at me and quietly said, "No ma'am."

I wish I'd just held him close and prayed over his life. I wish I had prayed with him and pleaded with God to remove the shackles that now held him in bondage. I wish I had told him about true repentance—hating one's sin so much that he or she will turn away from it.

CHAPTER 8

*A*pril 18, 2007, I arrived home from work and looked across the street. I noticed our neighbor was home early and casually mentioned it to my husband—I was talking to him on the phone.

When I entered the house, I found that Devon wasn't home.

"Did your brother ride the bus?" I asked my son Jason.

"No ma'am."

I called his job to see if he was there. This was feeling like before, but I forced the negative thoughts and the thread of fear to the side. I wanted to give Devon the benefit of the doubt.

He wasn't there, but he had called in to say he would be late.

This did nothing to ease my apprehension.

When the job called back to say Devon never came to work—I asked for the number he called from.

He had called from my neighbor's house.

I hung up the phone and told my husband.

He went over and knocked on the door.

No answer.

He knocked again.

Still no answer.

When he returned home, I told him that we should probably call the police since both of my neighbor's cars where parked in the driveway and because we knew our son had been in the man's house.

My heart was pounding hard in my chest.

Devon, what have you done this time?

The police arrived and we explained our son's history with the neighbor.

By this time, it was dark when they walked over and knocked on the door. We watched as they looked around the house, flashlights shining through the windows. I'm trembling all over by this time.

After about ten minutes, the officer returned to tell us that no one answered the door, but that she saw someone laying on the floor when she looked through the back door. She stated they were going to make a call so they could enter the house.

The crime scene investigation unit arrived.

I tried to swallow my panic as I thought about what was going on at that house and the fact that Devon was nowhere to be found.

After an hour, the female officer returned to confirm our worst fears. They had a body.

I immediately began crying and hollering, "Oh my God… no…"

My husband was still listening to her, but I couldn't hear anything.

She approached me and asked, "Ma'am, did you not hear me? It's not your son."

I look at her through my tears like she is crazy. My son wasn't the one dead, but he was in that house and there was a body. If he wasn't dead, then that meant he may have killed someone. It was all the more reason for my tears.

She gave us her card and encouraged us to call her if we had any more questions or ideas where my son may be.

My son taking a life? It was all too much to bear.

* * *

THE NEXT DAY, we received a phone call that they had arrested Devon and charged him with first degree murder. It was hard to believe that just nine days after my son's 17th birthday, he was a murder suspect. My heart has never hurt so bad. It felt like someone had just stabbed me, twisting the knife over and over.

When we went to court the following Friday for his arraignment, I thought I would get to see him but no, they were in another place on a TV monitor. I have never cried so much in all my life.

When it was his turn, they asked him if there was anything he wanted to say, "Is my dad here?"

We stood up.

"I'm sorry and I love you," is all he said to us.

I just cried and cried as we left the court room.

That next morning, I heard a lawnmower going. I was excited because every Saturday morning, our neighbor would get up and cut his grass.

It was just a dream.

I ran to the window and looked out.

My face dropped.

It wasn't that neighbor, but another one who had decided to cut his grass.

"We have to move," I told my husband. "There's no way I can continue to live on this street after all that had happened." It was just too painful—a sad reminder of all that was lost.

CHAPTER 9

a year later, Devon went to trial in August.

It was so hard to listen to the details of this case, but we had to be there to support our son.

We found out that Devon had still been in the house when his dad was knocking on the door. Evidence showed that he made calls to a girl and discussed their prom arrangements; he beat the neighbor with a bat, shot him twice, then covered him with a sheet and laid in his bed for several hours before leaving.

The prosecutor stated this was a premeditated crime. He said Devon bought a gun and waited for the neighbor to come home so he could rob him and kill him.

All of this testimony had my mind spinning.

There was no way they could be talking about my son. It had to be a dream and I just wanted to wake up. My neighbor's family sat on the right side of the court room crying as they heard all the details of the case. It was sad to think that his six-year-old daughter would never get to see her father again.

At the end of the week, my son was convicted of first

degree murder and breaking and entering. He was sentenced to four years for the breaking and entering and life with no parole for the first degree murder at the age of eighteen.

Our neighbor's family did not rejoice in this—they were just as sad as we were—there were no winners in this tragedy.

Before the court was dismissed, the judge asked if we had anything to say.

With tears running down my face, I said, "I'm so sorry this happened, but I still don't believe my son did this."

They embraced me and we stood in the middle of aisle crying.

My heart was broken.

Later that night, I received a call from my son stating that he was going to be transported in the morning. He repeatedly apologized and told me how much he loved me.

There were no winners at all.

wo years later, my son called and said, "Mom, I've started preaching the Word of God and leading people to Jesus. Mom, the only problem is no one wants to really listen to me because of the reason I'm in here. I feel like I am leading with a limp."

"Devon, you are doing what God called you to do at the age of twelve. No matter what people think, you just keep doing what you're supposed to do. God would prefer we have an occasional limp than a perpetual strut," I told him.

"Thank you Mom, for always encouraging me and pushing me through."

Every time my son sends a letter home he writes about his relationship with God and how he wants us to have that same relationship. He sends me Bible verses, asks me to pray with him on certain days and encourages me.

I received a letter from my son recently where he stated that when he was being taken out the court house during the trial—he looked back at me and he saw all the pain on my face that he had caused, but more than anything, he saw the love I had for him. He thanked me for being his mother when his biological mother was not there.

The day after I received the letter he called home. We discussed what he had written and I told him that during the trial, I felt L.I.M.P: lost, inadequate, mad and pain.

Over the years, I've sent encouraging cards to the guys that my son ministers to—they send me thank you cards. My son started taking classes to become a minister. He leads Bible classes and preaches every Wednesday. When my twelve-year-old son told me he was called to preach, I never thought that at age twenty-six, he would be in prison for life, preaching the word of God. Despite the path he chose, I know Devon's trial has truly turned into a triumph.

SHAVONNA FUTRELL IS Vice President of Victorious Ladies Reading Book Club, Shavonna was born in North Carolina and raised in Panama City, Florida. Shavonna is a mother of three adults and a wife of 21 years, she is an avid reader, loves to play bingo and spend time with her family, friends and sisters of her book club. You can contact Shavonna at: ShavonnaFutrell@gmail.com.

ELEVATION: LIVING LIKE AN EAGLE & NOT LIKE A PIGEON

MICHELLE CHAVIS

Scripture often refers to the eagle as a symbol of this renewing process. Psalm 103:5 says that, "our youth will be renewed like the eagle."

Youth, I believe, refers to the original image that God created us to be - His Love, His Wisdom and His Power. As we renew our minds, it's true. We'll be transformed back into God's image, which is what God intended for us all along.

One of the reasons I believe God uses the eagle as a symbol of this transformation process is that the eagle is the only bird whose whole physical strength is literally renewed after each molting season. In other words, only after the eagle has "put off" his old feathers, so to speak, does he actually receive "new" physical strength to soar above his enemies.

And it's the same with us. When we "put off" the old and "put on" the new, we too receive God's supernatural strength to soar above our enemies (Isaiah 59:19).

Another reason I believe God uses the eagle as a symbol of our renewal and transformation is because the eagle again comes from the only bird family that has "telescopic sight," a kind of "zoom-in-focus" lens. An eagle can search out objects literally miles away (indistinguishable to the human eye). Eagles can see a quarter from over 200 yards away and a rabbit from over a mile away. This, of course, increases their ability to judge and discern the true situation.

It's the same with us. Our minds, when renewed by God's Spirit, have the same supernatural ability. We are able to judge, discern and pick up things that the natural eye (natural mind) would never be able to see or understand. We are given the supernatural wisdom and ability to discern the true situation and see everything that happens to us from God's vantage point.

Pigeons eat seeds, while Eagles eat fish, turtles and snakes. Think about it—their digestive tracts are not the same; a pigeon can't handle what an Eagle can. When you choose to live as an Eagle, you will be ready to digest some things (trials and tribulations) that a pigeon couldn't handle.

"They that wait upon the Lord shall renew their strength; they shall mount up with wings like eagles; they shall run, and not be weary; and they shall walk, and not faint."

Isaiah 40:31

BROKEN HEARTS STILL BEAT

> Though He slay me, yet will I trust Him. Even
> so, I will defend my own ways before Him.
>
> *Job 13:15*

The Fourth of July was a time of year that I looked forward to celebrating and eating deliciously grilled food. However, it would become the catalyst of my heart crumbling into pieces.

This particular holiday began with a phone call from my aunt.

"Michelle, your daddy is gone, baby…"

My mind could not accept what I heard with my ears. "What do you mean?" I refused to even let the thought enter into my brain.

"He's gone, baby. He had a massive heart attack early this morning."

Nooo. There was some kind of mistake.

My aunt continued. "They're keeping his body here until you can get here."

Tears welled up in my eyes and overflowed, streaming down my face. "Daddy gone?"

Another thought entered my mind. My children. I have to tell them that their grandfather's gone.

I was sobbing as I called out for my children—my babies. While other families were celebrating the holiday—for us, the day was stained with tragedy. We would be dealing with the fireworks of our emotions.

I gave my children the heartbreaking news and offered what comfort I could provide. We were all in pain, hurting, and grieving the loss of my daddy.

Although not prepared mentally or emotionally, we arrived at my father house and proceeded to go to his room.

He lay there lifeless and helpless.

I think this is when reality set in for me and I began to feel regret for so many things—things I would have done differently; so many things I wish I had said to my father.

It was too late.

I would never hear my dad say, "Listen, do you understand me" or emphasize the pronunciation of his name: Benjamin BULLOCK.

My dad… daddy was now a memory on this earth. This handsome, always well-dressed man had stepped out of time into eternity. Now I had to push my pain aside and prepare to say a final goodbye to the man who gave me life.

In the midst of preparing for the home going celebration of my dad, I was hit with another blow to my heart. My maternal grandfather, Elam Chavis was ill, and had taken a turn for the worse. This news left me sorrowful because he and I shared a special bond. Some family members often teased that I was his favorite granddaughter. The simple truth is that I loved him and he loved me.

Four days after the death of my father, I received another

phone call—my grandfather made his transition on July 8th. Once again, I had to sit my children down and give them the sad news that another family member was gone.

As I mentally prepared myself to do the obituaries of both my father and grandfather, I prayed earnestly for God to give me the strength to endure the task of burying two men I loved deeply. I reminded myself constantly of the special memories I created with each of them, each one bringing me a small measure of joy for the time I was given to spend with my father and grandfather.

My father was buried on July 10th. God did not fail me during this time—He was my strength and my comforter. Praise God! However, my heart was still steeped in sorrow as I grieved for both my dad and my granddad.

The morning of my grandfather's funeral on the 13th, I was awakened from a nightmare by a phone call from my friend Toya. The dream was so disturbing that it left me with heart palpitations.

"I just had the worst nightmare of my life."

"What happened?"

"I dreamt that my mother passed." I couldn't stop my body from trembling—the dream seemed so real. "I walked in the room and saw her laying there covered with a pink sheet."

"Michelle, calm down. You've been through a lot lately."

I considered her words and decided not to tell anyone else—mostly because I was scared and I honestly didn't want to have thoughts of losing my mother. I took a moment to compose myself because my grandfather's funeral was in a few hours. I also spent time in prayer because I was concerned about my mother—she was close to her father and I worried about the effect his death might have on her health. She suffered from chronic obstructive pulmonary disease

(COPD), a type of lung disease which affected her airflow and resulted in my mother having to be on oxygen 24/7.

Despite her condition, my mom had always been a worshipper and a BOLD woman of God. She didn't care where she was, she was going to glorify God and give him praise. This didn't change during her father's funeral. She stood up praising God and waving her hands. It was as if she was basking in the presence of God.

Losing her father had taken a toll on my mom, however. My children and I ended up spending the night with her, the day after the funeral because she wasn't feeling well. She had her good and bad days, but you wouldn't know it to look at her or to hear her talk. Her faith in God was beyond measure.

* * *

THE FOLLOWING TUESDAY MORNING, my mom called me to inform me that she would be riding to Virginia so I didn't have to come up until later in the evening.

In our discussion, she mentioned finding someone to help me get a new washing machine—something I desperately needed.

Our call ended.

When my mom returned from Virginia later that afternoon, she called me and said, "I've arranged for someone to pick up the old washer so that the space will be ready when your new one arrives."

"Thank you, Ma," I replied.

"I told you that I was going to take care of you."

I smiled. Never was there any doubt in my mind that Mom wouldn't come through for me. She had always been my rock, my shoulder, my strength. She was everything a mother should be and more.

Two hours later, I was notified that Mom was having respiratory problems and the EMS had been called.

They were taking her to UNC.

While en route, I kept in touch to see where I needed to meet them.

My mother's condition was changing rapidly so the paramedics decided to take her to the nearest hospital, which was Granville Medical Center.

I immediately headed there.

Suddenly, the sky opened up and it began to storm—it was an angry one complete with lightning and thunder.

In the midst of the bad weather, a scripture dropped in my Spirit: "Though he slay me yet will I trust him." It provided me a measure of peace, which enabled me to get to the hospital without falling apart.

As soon as I arrived at the emergency room, I was informed that the ambulance had not arrived. At this point, I was getting frantic.

I struggled between worry, anger and lack of patience. I wanted to know what was going on. I wanted to see my mom; I needed to see her.

At some point, a nurse came to take me to see my mother. The ambulance had finally arrived. I breathed a sigh of relief.

But before she let me enter the hospital room, she said in a voice filled with sympathy. "I'm sorry but your mom didn't make it."

Tears rolling down my face in protest, I screamed in denial because this couldn't be true. I'd just spoken to my mom earlier that day. The nurse tried to console me, but I just wanted my mom.

I entered the room.

My beloved mother; my best friend was laying there beneath a pink sheet—the same one I had dreamt of just three days before.

I felt as if someone literally stabbed me in my heart.

My mother, my prayer warrior, intercessor, best friend, number one fan; encourager, and supporter—my mother was my EVERYTHING.

All I could think about was our last conversation and her last words to me: "I told you I was going to take care of you," and she had done that until she breathed her last breath on this earth.

This was by far the biggest trial of my life. I was already broken by the loss of my dad and grandfather, but on this day—Tuesday, July 16th, 2013, my heart had completely imploded into millions of pieces.

I had no idea what I was going to do or how I was going to do it, but I knew despite my emotional breakdown that God was going to get me through this pain, this heartache—this inconsolable grief.

I didn't eat for a few days. I cried until my eyes were swollen, but I kept reminding myself that I can do all things through CHRIST who exchanges strength with me.

I had to tell myself this even if I didn't feel it.

After talking with God, I began to look at my mom's transition from a different perspective.

I was sad, hurt, and angry because of all that had transpired while losing the three people dear to my heart within twelve days apart, but guess what?

I was still alive, not only that—my children were alive—not only that, we were all in our right mind with a reasonable portion of health and strength. This was a reminder that as bad as it was; it could have been worst. Although there were times I've been depressed, I learned to immediately say this scripture: *"Casting down imaginations, and every high thing that exalteth itself against the knowledge of God, and bringing into captivity every thought to the obedience of Christ."* This verse became a part of my daily living; a cue that I needed to keep my eyes on God and not focus on my grief.

In the midst of your pain, you have to know that God is still in charge and that He is our strength. If we give our heartache over to Him—He will help us navigate through the storms of life

MY PAIN PRODUCED MY PURPOSE

The Spirit of the LORD God is upon Me,
    Because the LORD has anointed Me to
    preach good tidings to the poor; He has sent
    Me to heal the broken-hearted, to proclaim
    liberty to the captives, And the opening of
    the prison to those who are bound.

Luke 4:18

We've heard the following quote many times: When life hands you lemons, just make lemonade. My response to this is: at least you can make different flavors!

Life is all about perspective. When we face trials and tribulations, we must learn to look at the bigger picture. The Bible teaches us in Philippians, Chapter 4: To be content in all things. Contentment brings a sense of peace and peace doesn't mean the absence of trouble but having the assurance that the same God that brought us through yesterday will bring us through today. We often sing the song: We've come this far by faith, leaning on the LORD, trusting in his holy WORD, he never failed me yet…

And He won't.

But do we really believe that? Or do we just sing the song out of repetition and or tradition. I've learned to count my rainbows, not my thunderstorms.

I hear the thunder, but I know who holds the sky. After the storm passes over, the sun will shine again. When the enemy shall come in like a flood, the Spirit of the LORD shall lift up a standard against him. (Isaiah 59:19).

I had to learn that my perspective of my predicament had to change. Yes, it was a tragedy to lose both my parents and my grandfather in a short period, but I reminded myself that I had many triumphs in which to glorify God.

Learning to find something good within a bad situation had to take place and that began with the transformation of my mindset.

Many of those days when my grief threatened to take over, I had to make affirmations and declarations over my life, because the enemy was after my mind. It was a daily process to tell myself that, "Depression cannot dwell in me, the number of my days God shall fulfil."

The strategy of the enemy is to have us like a pigeon, by planting thoughts in our mind, that we often manifest with our mouth. If it had not been for the pressing, shifting and beating in the Spirit, I would not be where I am today.

The Pruning Process was designed to develop me; not to destroy me. The Pruning Process was also designed to heal me; not to kill me. God is preparing me because "GREATER IS COMING."

One of my favorite scriptures that really helped bring me through this storm was Psalm 121: *I will lift up my eyes to the hills— From whence comes my help? My help comes from the LORD, who made heaven and earth. He will not allow your foot to be moved; He who keeps you will not slumber. Behold, He who keeps Israel shall neither slumber nor sleep. The LORD is your keeper; The LORD is your shade at your right hand. The sun shall not strike you by day, nor the moon by night. The LORD shall preserve you from all evil; He shall preserve your soul. The LORD shall preserve your going out and your coming in from this time forth, and even forevermore.*

SPEAK INTO THE ATMOSPHERE; TRAIN YOUR MIND TO HEAR WHAT GOD IS WHISPERING, INSTEAD OF WHAT THE ENEMY IS SHOUTING

Death and life are in the power of the tongue,
and those who love it will eat its fruit.

Proverbs 18:21

I am a chosen vessel, I am destined to be successful, I am above and not beneath, I am the head and not the tail; by the power of the blood I've been redeemed. I am not conceited, but I am convinced. With Christ in my life, I will always win, and no matter what, I will forever love the skin that I am in because I am a chosen vessel, and I'm destined to be successful.

I am strong in the LORD and in His mighty power. His grace is making me wiser and stronger. #declaration

Sickness cannot dwell in me, the number of my days God shall fulfill. God is watching over his WORD to perform it and Jehovah RAPHA is my healer. #declaration

I declare and decree I will not be moved by what I see but by my faith in God and His Word. I will see my situation through the eyes of God and every thought that exalts itself against the Word of God will be paralyzed in the name of JESUS! #declaration

The gift of God is stirred up in me therefore I shall live victoriously. #declaration

I walk in authority and everywhere my feet shall tread upon shall be blessed. #declaration

This is the day that The LORD has made and I will have abundance, excess and overflow in every area of my life. #declaration

Every wicked scheme and attack that attempted to come my way is paralyzed in the name of JESUS. #declaration

The Holy Spirit hovers me and the angels are protecting me I SHALL NOT FEAR! #declaration

I bind every thought that is contrary to the voice of God!! I am Kingdom-minded. #declaration

I have peace in the midst of my storm, because my mind is stayed on JESUS. #declaration

I serve a God who is able to do anything but fail, so his plans for me will always succeed. #declaration

If God be for me, the WHO doesn't matter, because God'S got me. #declaration

It doesn't matter what you say about me; God has already spoken over me. #declaration

I dwell in the secret place of the Most High (God), therefore I am protected from all hurt, harm and danger. #declaration

I will not worry but I will meditate on the word of God. #declaration

This is the day that the LORD has made and I will not have lack in any area of my life. My mind is renewed and my heart is receptive to the things of God. #declaration

I declare and decree that no weapon formed against me shall prosper Jehovah NISSI is fighting my battles for me. #declaration

I declare and decree that any thought contrary to the will of God be consumed and I will think on those things that are pure, lovely and of a good report. #declaration

I have a new mindset, new mercies, new thinking, new favor, renewed strength. I'm ready to conquer this day! #declaration

I declare and decree that this is the year of restoration, and all that I have sown in tears, I shall reap in joy. #declaration

DECLARE AND DECREE

I will bless the LORD at all times; His praise
shall continually be in my mouth. My soul
shall make its boast in the LORD; The
humble shall hear of it and be glad. Oh
magnify the LORD with me, and let us exalt
His name together. I sought the LORD, and
He heard me, and delivered me from all my
fears.

Psalm 34: 1-4

Father God, I come boldly to the Throne of
Grace.

Thanking You for who You are, God. LORD, You are
sovereign and worthy.

We magnify You and glorify You, LORD God.

LORD, You said in Your word, many are the afflictions of
the righteous, but You, LORD God will deliver us out of
them all.

LORD, execute every scheme and all wicked attacks that

are sent to destroy us. Bring all thoughts and negative mind-sets under subjection to you LORD God.

LORD thank you for your spirit of Boldness that We may speak with authority to those things that concern our lives in the atmosphere.

Your word says in Job 22:28 that we should decree a thing and it shall come to pass, so as we declare and decree these things we trust You and thank You for manifesting Yourself in every area of our lives.

I declare and decree that chains are broken, LORD God.

I declare and decree shackles are loosed, LORD God.

I declare and decree our minds are set free, LORD God.

I declare and decree peace in our life, LORD God.

I declare and decree that no weapon formed against us shall prosper, LORD God.

I declare and decree that we shall not die but live and declare the works of the LORD.

I declare and decree that we shall have faith like Abraham.

I declare and decree that we shall have wisdom like Solomon.

I declare and decree that we shall be obedient like Noah.

I declare and decree that your hedge of protection is covering us from all hurt, harm and danger.

I declare and decree that we shall have a victorious mindset.

I declare and decree that Jehovah NISSI is fighting our battles.

I declare and decree Jehovah JIREH is supplying our needs.

I declare and decree that Jehovah RAPHA is healing our bodies.

I declare and decree that we are the head and not the tail.

I declare and decree that we shall prosper even as our soul prosper.

I declare and decree that we shall walk in unity and love.

I declare and decree that the favor of God is upon us.

I declare and decree that we shall be made whole, mentally, emotionally and spiritually.

I declare and decree that you are the God of restoration and our faith is being restored.

I declare and decree that you LORD God will turn our trial into a triumph.

I declare and decree that we shall not be moved by circumstances, trials or adversity, because you are the Alpha and Omega, the author and finisher of our faith.

In JESUS Name.

Amen.

MICHELLE CHAVIS IS a native of Brooklyn, New York and now reside in North Carolina with her two children, Laticia and Trevon, whom she often refers to as her WHY. Michelle is a Director at Total Life Changes (TLC) and the President of Victorious Ladies Reading Book Club.

Michelle was recently awarded the 2016 Black Pearls Literacy Excellence Award. Her genuine, honest spirit allows people to feel comfortable talking to her about anything and some refer to her as their "Life Coach."

She is very passionate about helping people find their true purpose, and becoming their best. It is her desire to inspire and she is determined to leave a legacy and not just a headstone. You can contact Michelle at: mydesiretoinspireyou@gmail.com

LESS LIKELY TO SUCCEED

PATRICIA ALSTON-TAPP

Abuse and sexual assault can have a powerful impact on you and your relationships. It might be hard for you to trust anyone, even your own family members and you might feel dirty, disgusted, or even angry. Victims of sexual assault are six times more likely to suffer from post-traumatic stress disorder, which can lead to symptoms such as nightmares, feelings of emptiness, memory loss, guilt, shame, and loss of appetite.

Ultimately, rebuilding your life after you have experienced emotional, physical, or sexual abuse might be one of the most difficult things you will ever do, but it can also transform you in extraordinary ways if you acknowledge the challenges and work to heal yourself. Never let your past define your future.

*A*ndrea was swayed back and forth in the swing that hung from the old broken wooded porch. Every day she would come sit in this exact same spot, daydreaming— her favorite pastime. It was her way of taking her mind off of her situation. Otherwise, she would feel hopeless. Andrea was the third of five children born to a sugar cane factory-worker father and a stay-at-home mother.

When she was three, the family left Baltimore, Maryland, relocating to a small city in North Carolina. Her parents were devout Christians who taught their children strong Christian values. As far as Andrea could remember, attending church was never a choice but mandated.

Her father was a tall man; heavy built, and a strict disciplinarian. Her mother was a small frame woman, very beautiful with long silky black hair, soft spoken and a sweet humble spirit. It was evident that her father Alvin Greenwood was completely in charge and made all the major decisions in the home. He was the head of the house and this was as it should be—so I was taught. The fact that he was verbally and physically abusive toward her mother—Andrea didn't like it, but this had become their normal.

*A*s Andrea grew older, she watched in turmoil as her mother endured verbal, emotional, and physical abuse from her father. It only seemed to happen whenever he would drink, but the problem was that he drank every weekend. The assaults she witnessed produced mix emotions in her regarding her father. Whenever he came home at the end of the work week, Andrea would experience high anxiety, fear and anger because she knew what was about to unfold. She didn't like witnessing this treatment of her mother and vowed that no man would ever treat her this way.

She and her siblings often discussed the abuse, but never outside of the home—it was simply not done. Her parents had made it clear early on that whatever went on in the home—stayed there. Yet, deep down we knew that our mother lived in fear. Although she would never discuss it with us—I knew she wanted more out of life. Andrea didn't understand why her father was so cruel. Why he allowed himself to drink until it brought out the monster in him.

How could he mistreat his wife in front of their children?

She often wondered what he was thinking. Who would incur his wrath next?

It was this question that kept her on her toes. She wanted to be the good daughter—the one who stayed out of trouble. Andrea had dreams and she was intent on fulfilling each one of them. She would have her happily ever after. She didn't just want it for herself—she wanted it for her mother as well.

Andrea couldn't understand why her father treated her mother the way he did. Her mother was beautiful and smart. She was a good wife.

Whenever, she tried to broach the subject of her father's behavior, her mother would just make excuses for his explosive aggressive behavior.

"It's not him, it's the alcohol that makes him crazy. I'm trusting God for his deliverance," she would explain.

Andrea wasn't buying it.

Deep down to the core of her stomach, she resented her dad and her dislike of him threatened to consume her. Everything Andrea was taught in reference to honor and obeying her parents, she wanted to stomp and bury in the ground. She bottled up her emotions and locked them away. It was the only way to handle what she was dealing with.

CHAPTER 3

$\mathcal{B}$y the time Andrea was fourteen she had become an emotional wreck. She spent a lot of time crying, even when she didn't fully know why. In school, she often pretended everything was fine in her life when in reality—it was anything but okay. Thoughts of her mother constantly entered her mind, making her sad.

These racing thoughts were like a tape, playing over and over in her head. Andrea wondered if she was capable of finding love, leaving home and getting married. She still dreamed of living happily ever after.

One day while sitting in math class she drifted into her private thoughts. She didn't hear her math teacher, Mr. Lee, calling her name.

She snapped out of the daze as he approached her desk with a look of concern; for a moment she had to gain her composure.

As she looked around the class, everyone was staring at her, strange expressions on their faces. Andrea had no clue as to what was said or going on.

"Are you okay?" Mr. Lee asked.

"Sure," she replied. "Why you asking if I'm okay?"

"I called your name three times to get your attention. I want you to answer the equation problem on the board."

Andrea was embarrassed. She didn't know the answer. She hadn't been paying attention to what was going on in the classroom. Before she could open her mouth to say anything, the bell rang. The school day was over.

She breathed a huge sigh of relief.

Andrea grabbed her book bag and hurried out of the classroom, down the hall, out the door, and onto the bus.

She took her seat, her eyes gazed out the window and thought, *I was saved by the bell.*

The ride home was about twenty-five minutes which gave her some time to talk and laugh with friends.

Andrea had a group of friends who lived in the community. During the school week, they would all go home, do their chores and homework then meet up outside at the neighborhood basketball court, softball field or just hanging around in each other's yards.

Mostly Andrea was a very obedient child. She was respectful to both her mother and father. Even though there was dysfunction in the home, she and her siblings showed a lot of love and affection to one another. When her father was not on a drinking binge, he was very affectionate, attentive, and playful.

The family had difficult times and struggled financial, but God always made a way and they were able to survive their trials and the storms of life. They were taught that God was the answer to every problem. Her parents told her that God was Sovereign and the Almighty. Family prayer and Bible study was important and practice regularly in their home. Andrea knew that despite whatever happened, her mother always stood firm in her faith.

It was the foundation that would get Andrea through the rest of her life and the struggles that would come.

CHAPTER 4

*a*ndrea became a cheerleader in her freshman year at high school. She was excited about this and the fact that she had met an older boy named Rob. Her crush quickly developed into what she thought was love.

One night after a basketball game, they hooked up. While out together, he went into a club, leaving her in the care of one of his friends.

That *friend* raped her. He took advantage of Rob being in the club, forced himself on Andrea and then threatened her life if she ever told anyone.

She told Rob what happened, which led to a confrontation between the two.

Deep down, Andrea blamed herself for what happened.

The friend claimed that Andrea wanted it.

After that night, she tried to block it out and pretend that it never happened. Andrea was devastated, but she had to find a way to continue living.

She had no idea that what happened that night would continue to resurface throughout the rest of her life.

* * *

ANDREA NEVER TOLD anyone else outside of Rob.

She still wanted him despite everything and continued to see him. Their relationship eventually led to her getting pregnant.

By this time, he decided to enlist into the Army, leaving Andrea to deal with her pregnancy alone.

An abortion was out of the question.

Andrea was heartbroken. Why would Rob just leave her and their child like that? He told her that he loved her and she believed him.

Now she was all alone. An unwed mother-to-be.

What would her mother say? Her father... what would he do?

CHAPTER 5

*H*er parents were disappointed in her.

Andrea's father abruptly stopped talking to her. He told her that she was responsible for what had happened. Even her siblings treated her differently, although she knew they loved her. Andrea was going to have a baby and she felt isolated and alone.

She tried wishing it away, but it was futile at best.

As the months progressed, so did the child she carried.

Two months before her sixteenth birthday, Andrea gave birth to a beautiful baby girl she named Kayla.

She dropped out of school temporarily to take care of her daughter.

Her friends were doing their own things, going off to college, the military, etc. while she stayed at home playing mama. Even Rob was off enjoying his life with no attachments to her or the baby.

At this point in her life, all she ever heard was that, "You are never going to be anything … you made your bed hard so lie in it …"

Andrea didn't want this to be the end of her story, so she attended summer school and did everything she needed to do to graduate on time. She still had hope for the future, but soon found that life has a way of draining you of every ounce of happiness if you let it.

CHAPTER 6

*A*ndrea was eighteen years old with a two-year-old daughter. She had no job, no skills, no plan and couldn't see no way out. Her life seemed hopeless. Consumed with sadness and despair, and sinking into a deep depression, Andrea yearned to give up and run away. The only thing that kept her sane was the fear of what would happen to Kayla.

One night after she had put her daughter to bed, Andrea began pacing the floor, crying uncontrollable, and calling out to God for help.

She thought how her mother overcame all the pain and obstacles in her life. She never complained, her unwavering faith in God was a solid foundation firmly rooted. She would often say, "God won't put no more on you than you can bear. God *will* make a way."

Andrea knew that her mother never gave up hope. She vowed that she wouldn't give up either. She called on God and promised to put her faith in Him.

* * *

THE NEXT MORNING, Andrea's whole perspective changed. She began concentrating on God's goodness and everything she learned about Him growing up. She refused to let doubts, depression, self-pity and regret enter her mind.

"Today is going to be the best day of my life," she declared with tears rolling down her cheeks. "I trust you, Lord."

Andrea's confidence increased, and she was going to step out on faith as she had watched her mother do for many years.

With a new sense of determination and motivation Andrea made a decision to enroll in some classes at the community college. She asked her sister to babysit Kayla while she went through the enrollment process. After speaking with the counselor, financial aid and admission office personnel, Andrea felt pure joy and satisfaction.

She was going to college.

She did not have a car but getting to and from the college would be no problem because it was walking distance from her home.

Everything was falling into place.

She didn't have to worry about childcare because there was a program to assist with daycare and she qualified for it.

For the first time in years, Andrea had renewed hope for a brighter future.

When Andrea returned home, her sister was sitting in the recliner with a book. She went over and gently tapped her on the shoulder.

"Hi Sis," she said, "You're back already."

Andrea grinned from ear to ear. "Yep, everything went well. I will be starting classes next semester."

"That's great," Alicia replied. "What will you do with Kayla?"

"There's a childcare program available and I signed all the necessary forms today. I will be able to drop her off before class and pick her up at the end of the day. As long as I maintain a certain grade point average. I'm good."

"Well alright. I'm so happy for you, Andrea."

She was beaming and her face lit up like lights from a Christmas tree. Deep inside, she felt God heard her cry and was opening doors showing her. Andrea felt loved and that her life mattered to Him.

That night, Andrea fell to her knees and prayed. She thanked God for the new opportunities that she had been given and vowed she would live her life with purpose. She thought about the abuse her mother suffered, the rape and her feelings of unworthiness. She had suppressed those feelings for so long that she had begun to live in bondage of fear and failure.

In the following weeks, Andrea sought help from a nonprofit rape crisis organization. A few sessions in, she was able to talk about her traumatic ordeal and let go of the guilt and shame she had carried for so long.

Andrea gradually began to accept that she was not responsible for what happened to her. It was not her fault. She continued to go to the rape center and eventually began volunteering one day a week. Because of her personal experience, Andrea was able to help other rape survivors. She found that she had a passion for helping others. It was part of her ministry.

CHAPTER 7

*A*ndrea attended community college for two years while working a part-time job. Not only had God worked out her situation, but He had also stepped into her father's life, prompting him to stop drinking. He was now a better man and husband. She also had the support of her parents. Her mother kept Kayla while Andrea went to school at night.

She worked extremely hard, made excellent grades, and even made the Dean's list. Andrea later went to the University of Chapel Hill and graduated with honors with a degree in Social Work. After graduation, she landed a job with the Department of Social Services. She worked with low income families, domestic violence, and teen pregnancy. She became a mentor to many teen mothers, which she found very rewarding.

Andrea will tell anyone that she could not have done this without God. She also believes that had she not witnessed the abuse in her family and been raped—she may have taken a different path. Becoming a mother at an early age, forced her to grow up and live in the real world. There was no time for daydreaming. She was responsible for her daughter and Andrea wanted to do what was best for Kayla.

God had blessed her with her beautiful little girl as a reminder that He is the author of all things good. Despite the circumstances of her conception—Kayla was innocent and she was a gift—a gift from the Most High. Only He can turn a trial into a triumph.

Andrea's story is not my story, but it is one shared by many women. It is my prayer that her resilience and determination to be a survivor and not a victim, will inspire all.

PATRICIA ALSTON-TAPP IS an honorary member of the VLR book club and prayer warrior. Patricia is a wife, mother of three beautiful daughters, grandmother of six and great grandmother of four. She values and loves her family. Her message is sending Hope with the Word of God in any situation and life circumstances. She can be reached at pattapp03@gmail.com.

HOUSE OF LIES

NICHOLE PAGE

A woman will go through life praying for this to happen: great job, wonderful husband, beautiful home, and children. Well, that's the order I had planned for myself, but life took a different turn and darkness almost consumed me.

There are some situations in life that will cause you to snap in a way that you won't even recognize yourself.

PROLOGUE

I stood backed against the kitchen counter, tightly gripping the wooden handle of my ECKO Forge ten-inch, two-milimeter knife.

Sharpness, precision and perfection. They don't make these kind of knives like this anymore, I thought, twirling it.

The hot venom of fury poisoned my veins as I rocked back and forth, glaring at Him while filled with rage.

My grip on the knife—my psycho knife, was so tight that I'm sure my fingerprints were embedded for life. I had suddenly morphed into a monstrous being. It was as if I had left my body and was bearing witness to what was about to happen.

The kitchen—my kitchen had transformed into a place of anger, hurt, betrayal and pain. It was now the scene of what would be a horrific crime.

Oh God! Oh God! Please! What do I do?

CHAPTER 1

he phone was ringing off the hook.
It stopped.

Good.

I was busy and didn't have time to talk at the moment.

It rang again.

If someone was this insistent—maybe, I needed to answer.

I'm coming! I'm coming!

I eyed the caller ID, recognizing the name of a friend.

"Hello," I greeted.

"Hey, Nik... I'm sorry."

Sorry? About what? I was confused by her tone and her words. "What's going on, Tish?" I could feel in my spirit that something wasn't quite right. "Is everything okay?"

No answer.

"*Tish.*"

I'm here," she said, her voice cracking.

Was she crying? I wondered.

"Tish, what's wrong? Did Tony do something to you?" I

was determined to get to the bottom of this. "What's wrong? Say something... *please.*

"Tony and I had a heated argument. The kids were crying, begging us to stop yelling. He pointed his finger all in my face, cursing and all. Girl, he told me if I open my mouth he was leaving. I told him to leave.

"What did you guys argue about?"

"Nik, I really need to talk to you. Can you come over, please?"

"I'm on my way." My girl needed me, so I dropped everything and left my house to be with her.

When I pulled into Tish's yard, the kids were outside playing.

I noted that Tony's car was gone. Probably a good idea for him to leave with tensions running high.

Both of the girls yelled out, "Hi, Aunt Nikki!" and came running to give me a hug.

"Hi sweeties... is mommy in the house?"

"Yeah, she was crying," one responded. "Mommy and daddy were yelling at each other. Then he left." She paused a moment before asking, "Is my dad coming back?"

I didn't answer her question... just stared at her until her sister called her to return to the game they were playing. Grateful for the reprieve, I walked up the steps toward the front door.

I really had no idea what to expect, but I took a deep, calming breath and opened the screen door.

Tish lay balled up on the couch, eyes bloodshot red from crying. I never had seen her like this. Tony and Tish were usually the *fun* couple. Whenever we get together, they were always the life of the party. Tony was a comedian and a romantic. Always kissing Tish's hand or hugging her.

I would always tease him by saying, "Tony, Tish got you whipped... just a puppy wagging his tail for more."

They were a great couple to be around... always keep me laughing.

"What's wrong, Tish? What did Tony do?"

She placed her hand on top of mine hand and squeezed. This was not the Tish I know. The woman I knew was fearless; she wasn't one to beat around the bush—always upfront and honest.

Just seeing her in this way, brought tears to my eyes. "Tish, is it that bad? You can tell me and it will not go outside this room. I never saw you cry... talk to me."

Her head bowed, she placed a hand on top of mine. "Nik, what I'm about to say to you may change the way you feel about me... our friendship. I cannot keep this to myself any longer because it's wrong and eating me alive. It's about your husband, Brent."

I took a deep breath... just sighed, waiting for what was about to be announced to me.

"Nik, before I tell you this, I investigated everything myself. I needed to be sure. I'm so sorry, but you work your tail off trying to provide for you and Brent. Just had a house built and you took on a second job to furnish it. You work around the clock... it's not right."

I said nothing, yet confused, but still listening.

She gazed at me with tear-glazed-bloodshot eyes. I can see this was tearing her to pieces.

Her voice began to crackle as she festered up the words to say, "My co-worker and I was eating lunch. "Tish, you know everybody in this town. Do you know this guy named Brent Sanderson?"

I told her yes, I know of that name... describe him to me. She described him... a perfect match.

She continued to tell me where he worked.

I asked her, "What was his friend's name?"

"Tony."

A wave of shock overtook me. After I found my voice, I uttered, "That's my husband!"

She looked at me and said, "Really, makes a lot of sense."

"How do she know Tony and what do you mean by saying, *it makes a lot of sense?*"

Of course, I didn't budge, just registering everything Tish was saying to me. I controlled my breathing enough to listen to my heart beat…it hypnotized me for a minute.

"Nik! Nik!" Tish shouted.

"I'm listening to you."

She continued by saying this girl said that Brent and Tony were at a function over her best friend's house. I asked her the friend's name, but she didn't want to say. I then asked her what was the function and she said a small party. So, I wanted to know what our husbands were doing at a party—a party neither one of us knew about."

"What did she say?"

"This girl had the nerve to say the party was for her friend and Brent.

I asked her again, "So what kind of party was this?"

"An engagement party," she responded.

"Stop lying… that's impossible." Shaking my head, I questioned, "So who is he supposed to be marrying?"

Tish stopped talking and just stared at me.

I was puzzled, tongue-tied, completely in disbelief. I just sighed and shook my head. I placed my elbow on my leg, head bowed, massaging my temples. The only word that rolled off my tongue was, "hah." I didn't go into a rage because it seemed so far-fetched… just didn't seem real. This could not be real and happening to me. I stopped massaging my temples to look up at Tish.

Before I could mutter another word, she said, "Nik, there is more."

Seriously, it can't get any worse than this. Lord knows

what else can she say. I'm still trying to swallow everything that was said. My Brent... not my Brent. He would not do this to me. Maybe Tish's co-worker was just making this crap up. Maybe she had a little thing for him. But an engagement party... Really! Oh God! *Please*! This can't be happening to me!

"Nik, there is more. I'm so sorry, but I have to tell you this. You need to know the rest of this story."

But do I really want to know the rest of the story. Should I just get up and leave? Maybe just confront my husband?

"Are you okay?" Tish inquired. "I'm so sorry."

"Before you go any further, where is your husband?"

"I will get to his sorry, trifling tail. He is furious with me, but you best believe I'm not finish with him either."

Tish took a deep breath and puked up the words to say, "I asked for the woman's name. My co-worker didn't tell me right away. I had to keep after her, but I got it. Her name is Kiana. When I got home, I did some investigation on her before I confronted Tony. It's not good, Nik... not good at all... so sorry."

I took several deep breathes... my blood started to slowly boil. Tish wouldn't lie to me about things in my marriage. She noticed my disposition changed and becoming upset. I just stared off into space waiting to be punked... just want to laugh this off from being punked.

"Nik?"

My eyes met hers.

"This woman works at a daycare. You need to call this number and make an appointment for tomorrow to see the place. The address is on the back. Even though you don't have a child, act like you do. She's the director. She will talk to you in her office about the daycare than show you around. You must do this face to face tomorrow. It's unbelievable and it's not right but you have to do this."

I reached for the number and called in front of Tish.

It rang two times before someone answered with a friendly greeting.

It seemed like the longest greeting in the world. Hurry, so I can get this over with.

"Hello, my name is Nichole Page. *I used my maiden name to avoid being suspicious.* I'm interested in enrolling my child in your daycare. Is it possible if I can make an appointment for tomorrow?"

The receptionist... I assumed it was the receptionist said, "Yes, that will be wonderful. Are you available to come at three p.m.?"

Oh yes, this will be a perfect time for me. I was looking forward to meeting this woman.

CHAPTER 2

I left work at two-thirty, and headed to the daycare. As I was driving, I felt my body temperature rise... fire and rage building up... my head felt like it was about to explode. Another woman. My husband didn't just have a side chick—he had a fiancée. This was straight out of a *Lifetime* movie.

I struggled to gather my thoughts and get myself together as I drove into the parking lot of the daycare.

I pulled into the parking space, placed the gear in park and stared into space.

After a moment, I called Tish.

"Please pick up the phone," I whispered.

"Hello."

"Tish, it's Nik. I'm at the daycare but haven't gone inside yet. I don't think I can do this. Girl, I'm scared I might go in here and explode. I just might get arrested."

"You can do this," my friend assured me. "This isn't right and you don't deserve this. Just go in, prepare yourself; listen and don't get arrested.

I wasn't sure I could make that promise.

I walked into the daycare and a receptionist greeted me. "Hello, may I help you?"

I quickly scanned her. She had a cute face. Maybe this was the fiancée. No, Tish said she was the director.

"Yes, I have an appointment to enroll my child and tour the facility...Nichole Page." "Oh yes, Ms. Watts is expecting you. Please have a seat."

The receptionist picked up the phone and announced, "Your three o'clock just arrived."

The door across from me opened.

A very homey, pleasant woman stepped out wearing a gold button-up, red and black flowery shirt, black slacks, pearl studs, and very dark plum color lipstick... not exactly what I expected. Her hair was a little messy on one side... maybe she was playing with the children. I mean I'm no Tyra Banks or Hallie Berry, but good Lord...*are you serious*! She looked hard and run down like that old saying, "Old race horse, rode hard and put away wet."

This cannot be the fiancée.

"Hello Ms. Page," Kiana Watts said, extending her hand. "Welcome to our daycare."

I shook her hand.

"Please follow me into my office."

It couldn't get any worse with the thick southern accent. So, I followed.

She led me through, shutting the door behind us.

My eyes were fixated on her not noticing anything else.

"Please have a seat and again, welcome."

I took my eyes off of her to sit down. When I looked up, I was shocked, lost for words. This cannot be...I'd just stepped into the *Twilight Zone*.

My teeth grinding, eyes constantly scanning the objects before me. I just could not believe what I was seeing. The bookshelf had framed family pictures.

I slowly rose to my feet and moved to get a better look at the pictures.

Ms. Watts interrupted my thoughts by saying, "Those are pictures of my fiancé and our children." One picture was of a baby boy and the other of a little girl. The other picture consisted of this man holding a little girl with a tutu on.

As I brought my head closer to the picture of the man and little girl—it was my jerk of a husband or he had an identical twin.

I backed away from the shelf in complete shock.

"Ms. Page, are you okay?"

I could not say a word. I took a step backwards to feel for the chair then turned around. Right above the chair was a large family portrait of him, her, and their children. I immediately felt sick to the stomach. My God, I wanted to snatch that portrait off the wall and beat her with it, but I kept my composure. I was going to get an explanation.

"Ms. Page, are you okay? Do you need any help?"

I just stared at her for a minute.

As if sensing my fury, she took a step back.

"No, I don't need help. But I would like to know why my husband is in these pictures? *What is going on*? No worries and no need to call security. I'm not going to act like a lunatic unless I have too plus there are children in the building. I just want the truth."

"You're *his* wife? Oh My God!"

I noticed that her eyes were beginning to fill with tears.

"This can't be right. Brent has never been married. Oh My God! We live together and have two beautiful children. I mean, we do everything together." The woman was talking nonstop. "The longest we broke up was about a year, but still remained friends… sometimes intimate. He is so close to my family. They love him. Before you arrived, I was making arrangements with vendors for our wedding in a month. I just got off the phone with the pastor at my church."

She grabbed some tissue from her desk to wipe her eyes, took a deep breath and sat back into her chair. She was distraught, repeating herself, "Brent is my fiancé. We have been together, off and on, for the past eight years."

So, he was with this woman before we got married.

She continued, "We have a four-year-old daughter and 10-month old son."

I thought to myself this jerk made children with another woman during our marriage, and got engaged... I WANT TO KILL HIM!

"Ms. Watts, I have questions and need answers. I'm doing everything in my power to keep it together. Currently, Brent is married to *me*. We are not separated nor divorced. I guess he don't know that he can go to jail for bigamy. I'm pretty sure you don't want his children to be fatherless. *Please, enlighten me.* I need to know what the heck is going on and handle this."

I repositioned my body in the chair, propped my elbow on the arm rest, raised my hand to rest my head. My eyes traveled to the rock on her finger.

It was bigger than mine.

I muttered a string of curses in my head.

My blood was straight boiling now, but I had to hold it together. "Ms. Watts, when did he propose to you?"

She nervously responded, "Brent, proposed to me a couple of weeks ago in front of my staff. It was amazing. The staff knew of the engagement surprise. When it was time for lunch, some of the staff and I walked down to the break room. I was shocked to see Brent there wanting to have lunch with me. He then asked for everyone's attention, got down on one knee, and asked me to marry him."

For some strange reason, I felt like she slightly enjoyed

talking about her engagement; then, I could be wrong. This was disgusting... absolutely disgusting. I fought back the tears. First of all, I could not believe what I was seeing... now what I'm hearing. I honestly wanted to puke.

There was a moment of silence.

"Keep going, Ms. Watts. I'm sure there's more."

She glared at me. I guess she wasn't expecting me to say that.

"Wait a minute!" I said. "Something is not adding up. Did I hear you say you and Brent are living together? How in the world is that possible when we share a home?"

"Brent, most of the time is with us in the evening. Recently, that has changed because his father moved out. He needed to be there for his mother at nights."

Hmmm... that's probably because I just stop working third shift.

"Brent and I work the same schedule except he gets off at two hours early to pick up the kids. I don't get off until five sometimes later. He calls to let me know he got the kids and heading home. They are fed and bathed by the time I get home. We do everything together."

What was that supposed to mean? Really! Oh this witch is definitely not leaving this office till I get everything I need. "Hold up, this is a bunch of crap. Brent calls you from where and picks the kids up in what?"

She sarcastically says, "He calls me from his cell phone and picks the kids."

Swelling with anger, I asked, "In what...in his Maxima? And what cell phone?"

She boldly states, "Brent and I share cellular family plan."

I glared at her. "Brent doesn't own a cell phone."

She continued to say, "He drives our babies in their car seats in his car."

"*Car seats.*"

"Yes. He has a booster and baby car seat in his car. I have

the same in my car."

I gagged, saying, "I have never seen car seats in his car nor seen him carrying a cell phone."

She even looked puzzled.

I absorbed every word that rolled from her tongue. *Numbed, humiliated, and so disgusted. I'm going to kill him.*

She reached to the bottom of her desk drawer and pulled out a small, thick photo album book.

I will truly throw up in her lap if I see another picture. Is she really about to hand me this album? God, I wish I had a match to burn every picture.

With a slight smirk on her face, she handed me the album. "This album has pictures of us vacationing and our children. I have the originals at home. I keep this one at work because it gets me through stressful days."

Looking down at the book... did she just say *vacations*! I bluntly interrupted, "Did you say vacations?"

She replied, "Yes. We vacation at least twice a year in Florida. My sister goes to college there and we take Kaitlyn to Disney."

He does go deep sea fishing with friends in Florida a couple of times a year.

My vision blurred from the tears gathering in my eyes. I did not want to open this book but I did. I slowly flipped through each page beginning with Brent, her, and their child in front of a resort followed by pictures with Disney characters, and random pictures of them having fun.

Next, I flipped to a picture of her pregnant in a hospital bed with Brent sitting in a chair. The next picture was Brent cutting the umbilical cord of a baby with the date and time stamped on it. It felt like a dagger to the heart.

That's the date we closed on our house but he had a case that afternoon.

The tears finally fell.

CHAPTER 3

"Oh God. Take the book. I'm going to be sick."

As I bowed my head in the chair, she said, "I'm sorry, but I didn't know he was married. I don't know what else to say. I've always loved Brent. He made me the happiest woman alive when he proposed. We have two beautiful children. Soon we will be married and moving into our new home. I'm sorry... I love him."

The phone on her desk began to ring.

I glared at her as she looked at the caller ID. It seemed like she was barely able to breath.

The phone rang again.

"Is it Brent calling?"

She nodded yes.

"Answer the phone and put it on speaker. I promise I won't not say a word."

She seemed nervous and hesitated to do it initially, but after a moment she agreed. "Hey, hun!"

Is she really trying to add fire to my rage?

I could hear Brent saying, "I picked up the kids and I'm

about to grab something through drive-thru and head home. Do you want anything to eat?"

She replied, "No!"

"Well, I see you when you get home… love you."

She choked up, "Love you, too."

Then she pressed the speaker button and ended the call.

I lost it… I needed to get out of there before I ended up in jail. I don't know who angered me the most.

I got up from the chair, stood up, and used my sleeve to wipe my tears. *Don't make a scene… don't make a scene.* Lord knows, I wanted to destroy her office, shove every picture down her throat, wrap that phone cord around her neck, and choke the life out of her. This witch actually had the nerve to say, "Love you too" in front me. As if everything was just fine. Didn't she hear anything I'd said. The man was *my husband*.

I took a step toward her desk, leaning forward. "I'm done… you can have him."

I stormed out of her office.

My adrenaline was so ramped up, I thought the glass cracked in the door, as I forcefully exited the building.

Hysterically crying, I got into my truck shouting, "I'm going to end his life."

CHAPTER 4

While driving, tears made a river down my face and snot poured from my nose. I came to a red light and cried harder.

A horn squealed in protest behind me.

I jumped. I was almost home. *Just let me make it home without accident.*

Finally, I see my driveway and pulled into the garage. *I usually don't park in the garage... Brent does... surprise him.*

I walked into the house and laid my purse on the kitchen island, then headed to the bathroom to clean my face and blow my nose. I could not stop crying. *I trusted this man, was faithful to him, and truly loved him. I work my tail off... two jobs to provide. I thought we were going to have a child. He stripped all of that from me.*

The phone rang.

I walked over to look at the caller ID.

It was Tish.

I slowly reached for the phone to answer. It felt like my throat closed up, tears falling from my eyes saying, "Hello... Tish. Oh God! Tish, I just can't..."

"Nik, I'm so sorry. I didn't want you to hurt. But you had to see it. That's why Tony is staying with his mother. He told me I should've minded my own business; You know I told him where to go. Girl, we had a terrible argument. But I had to tell you because you work too hard. Please stop crying. The kids and I are coming over."

I felt numb all over... except when it came to my heart. It had shattered like a broken mirror in millions of glass shards.

"Tish, I'm not myself right now. I need to be alone and wait for Brent to walk through this door. He is going to see a side of me he has never encountered before. I'll call you when I'm through with him."

"Nik, just don't do... I'm sorry... everything will be okay."

I hung up the phone. I wasn't in the mood for any more conversation. There was no way Tish could talk me out of my rage.

I walked back into the kitchen and leaned against the island crying.

I turned to look at the microwave clock.

It was almost eight o' clock.

Minutes later, I heard the garage door go up; then back down. *I guess he was surprised to see my truck in the garage.*

I opened my knife drawer to grab my "Psycho knife." I placed the knife behind me waiting for him to walk in my direction.

The sound of the front door opened. The footsteps got louder as he approached the kitchen.

White hot fury took over.

It was like slow motion as Brent came into the entrance of the kitchen.

We were face to face.

"Nik, why are you crying?"

"You *know* why I'm crying," I yelled.

He looked shocked and confused. "What are you talking about?"

Is he serious! This jerk is really taking me for a joke! My blood boiling, "Who is Kiana Watts?"

With a straight look on his face, "Nik, I don't know who you're talking about."

Clinching the handle of my knife behind my back shouting, "Boy, you better come correct and you better come quickly."

He took a few steps towards the refrigerator.

I stepped around the island to block him in.

His voice jumped a pitch, "Nik, you need to calm down."

Before I knew it, I had my knife about three inches from his throat.

All of a sudden he became paralyzed with fear, saying, "Put the knife down before someone gets hurt."

Rage swept over me and my vision blurred with tears, "I will cut your head off and present it to her and your precious children. Don't play… *Speak!* You been keeping a lot of secrets… telling me lies so you *better* tell me the truth right now. So help me, God; you will feel this blade penetrate through your neck."

Seconds passed.

His eyes twitched from the blade to me. "Kiana and I are just friends. We were friends before I met you."

He was telling me a boldface lie to my face. "You're lying. Let me correct you," I said. "She is not your friend; *she is your fiancée.* You have a four-year-old daughter and a ten-month old son. You take vacations to Florida. Plans are being made for a wedding in a few weeks. Tony… best man and your brother… groomsman… Next, a new home. I hope you all burn in hell."

As I dangled the blade in his face, he stepped backwards. He's probably thinking to run for it, but I interrupted his thought by saying, "Don't even think about it," I warned. "My aim is good. You best believe this blade will be through the back of your neck before you reach that front door. Oh, by the way, I saw the pictures in her office of your cute little family.

He looked surprised as the color drained from his face.

My rage was intensifying. "I listened to every word you said when you called her office including how much you loved her and that you were going to McDonalds to pick food for your children."

Brent stood there, guilt written all over his face. I'm sure he wanted to disappear. My blade was still inches from his neck.

"Talk," I yelled.

He gagged up the words to say, "Nik, I'm sorry. I never meant to hurt you. Please lower the knife."

I lowered the blade parallel to my hip, but still pointed to his abdomen. Thinking to myself, I'm going to gut his tail like a fish if the truth is not told. He repeated, "I never meant to hurt you."

Tears rolled down my cheek as I looked him in the face. I uttered, "So, when is the wedding?"

"I'm married to you and I love only you. I was never going to marry her. I gave her the ring because she was nagging me about all the years we've been together and having a solid relationship for our children. So I proposed to shut her up. A wedding was never going to take place."

He truly disgusts me.

I continued to say, "You made not only one child, but two in our marriage. Do you know how sickening it was to see pictures of you and the illegitimates? It was a dagger to the heart seeing you cut the umbilical cord of your son then the next picture all cuddled in the hospital bed together. I had to jog my memory. That cutting of the cord picture was stamped with a date on it. It was the date we closed on our house and were moving boxes in. I remember you telling me that you will be called in for a case. So now that I think about it, your case was your baby being born. Better yet, your job is your alibi when you disappear for hours to be with them. I practically work around the clock while you're playing me."

His eyes looked down at the blade as I turned the handle a few times. I reassured him by saying, "No worries right now, I will kill you in a few minutes... just answer the questions."

"It was accident when she got pregnant."

I spit out, "Oh let me guess, she walked, tripped, and landed right on you naked. It happened at least twice during our marriage. Do you know you could have given me a STD or worse... AIDS?"

He nonchalantly replied, "Nik, she's clean."

I snapped and uttered a string of curses that would make a sailor blush. I should go in the garage, grab my steel bat, and bash your skull open for saying that crap."

"Where are the car seats and cell phone because they're not in your car?" I demanded.

"I keep the car seats and phone in a small storage unit by the job. When I get off, I go by there to get the seats and phone then pick up the kids."

It took everything in me to control my arm from cutting him at that moment.

"Nik, please," he begged, "I'm sorry."

I raised my arm, with the blade, to wipe my tears with the sleeve. "So, the times you told me you were going deep sea fishing with friends in Florida, you guys were vacationing a Disney."

He replied, "Yes and we picked her sister up for school break."

"I work my tail off... third shift at the hospital and first shift at a research lab. I couldn't figure out why you were always so broke. The money you borrowed to get your car fixed was to get her a car... right?"

"She was having car trouble and her car is old. Our babies needed to get to appointments and school. I was going to give it back."

"You're taking my money, giving it to her, and spending it on *them*." I was transforming into a wild animal, infested with rabies, screaming and crying. "You know, for the life of me, I never could understand why women snap especially when it comes to trifling men. *Now, I know why*! Do you want to know, Brent? Do you want to know why? Why? You played me really bad for five years. My trust, you killed it... happiness, you destroyed. Now it's your turn."

He seemed like he was barely able to breathe and whimpered, "I'm sorry, Nik. Please give me another chance. I love you so much."

I was deaf to his words... meaningless.

Backed up against the counter, tightly gripping the wood handle of my ECKO Forge ten-inch, two-milimeter thick blade... my Psycho knife.

"They don't make these kind of knifes anymore, twirling it... sharpness and perfection."

I was completely furious, veins poisoned with rage... rocking back and forth... just glaring at him. The grip was so tight that I'm sure my fingerprints were embedded for life. I morphed into a monstrous being... so much rage and pain.

Oh God! Oh God! Please! What do I do?

My body locked up with fury, gripping tightly, I rose by blade. Suddenly, I envisioned my parents saying, "Don't do it, baby. Don't throw your life away over a *Nothing*. He's not worth it."

I lowered my blade as bowed my head.

Looking him in the face, "You need to get out of this house quickly. It's taking everything in me not to bury my blade in your throat. I truly advice you to leave my presence. *Leave now!*"

"Nik, this is my house too. I want to work things out. I don't love her… never did. I was just giving her what she wanted to here and did everything she wanted me to do, so it will never come back to you. I love my kids that I have with her. You will learn to love them too. Look, I was going to tell when the time was right. Nik, we can start a family of our own. Please…"

In a harsh tone, I stated to him, "You did this in the dark, you keep them in the dark."

The words that rolled off his tongue meant nothing to me.

Everything was a lie! This house was built on a lie! Our marriage… a lie!

With my blade pointed downwards, I raised my head to look him in the eye. Feeling anger swelling in me, I said, "You performed an unspeakable act. You crossed me. Now, I wipe my hands of you. Do not say another word to me nor get in my way. I want you out of this house before I return from Jersey."

Tightly gripping the handle of my blade, I turned away from him and headed upstairs. I packed my duffle bag, swung it over my shoulder, grabbed by blade, and ran down the steps.

When I entered the kitchen to get my purse off the counter, Brent was sitting on the couch like a statue.

God, I wish I had some gasoline to throw on him and light his behind up.

I picked up speed to get out of there.

I put my bag in the back seat of my truck, blade and purse on the front passenger seat, opened the garage door and left.

No looking back.

CHAPTER 5

*I*t was a long ride on Interstate 95, but I was determined to get to Jersey.

I finally arrived at my parents' home.

Looking in the rear view mirror did not help. Look at my face! Eyes blood shot red and puffy! I need to clean myself up before I ring the doorbell. They have no idea what happened or that I'm here.

I grabbed my purse, slid my blade in my duffle bag, walked to the door, and listened to the sound of the doorbell.

What a beautiful sound.

Daddy answered the door. He was excited to see me saying

"Hey baby! What a nice surprise! What are you doing here?"

I hugged and kissed him on the cheek. Extending his hand, "Give me your bag. Mommy is in the kitchen. She's cooking breakfast and baking chicken for tomorrow's dinner. Better yet, she's drying out chicken. Ready to eat some leather?"

Daddy always makes me smile and laugh. He is a God-fearing, loving man… spiritual and philosophical.

Mommy came out the kitchen.

Surprised to see me, "What are you doing here this early in the morning? I talked with you this morning on your way to work. You look so tired and shouldn't be driving so late at night by yourself. Did Brent come with you?"

Before I could answer, Daddy said, "Baby, before we start talking I want to pray with you. Thy Heavenly Father, I want to thank you for bringing my baby to us safely and without harm. Continue to bless her, Lord. Whatever burden she seems to be carrying… remove it. In your precious name, Lord, Amen." He paused a moment before saying, "Nikki, I love you and miss you." Dad must have noticed the burden I was carrying.

At that moment, I cried a river.

With concern in his voice, Daddy asked, "Baby, what's wrong? You would have not driven eight hours, if nothing wasn't bothering you."

Mom, quickly answered, "Brent!"

My parents stared at me as I reached into my bag and grabbed my blade. They were shocked.

Mommy said, "What happened? Did you kill him?"

Dad slightly tilted his head and smoothly said, "Everything will be just fine. We will handle it."

I was crying and sobbing telling them what happen from beginning to end. I reassured them that Brent was alive but he came very close to decapitation.

Mom just shook her head saying, "Honey, you're better than me. That knife would have been shoved down his throat coming out the other end of his tail!"

Crumbling inside, I mumbled, "You guys saved him. With that blade clinched in my hand, I was ready to dive into his neck. But I saw your faces and heard your words that brought me here."

That moment was a turning point in my life. There was no going back to lies, stress, and misery.

I stayed with my parents for the rest of the week.

During my time at home, Dad prayed for me and with me. I was so disappointed in myself for not catching any of his acts which led me to cry myself to sleep at night.

They encouraged me to be a solid rock...head strong, patient, and continue to use my 'street smarts' and common sense. Dad reminded me that my marriage could be annulled because of Brent's actions.

It was my last day with my parents.

As I was showering, I had one last cry. Those tears from him blended with the water headed to a point of no return.

I didn't want to leave but I had to head back to what was now hell for me. I packed my clothes and blade in my bag, and then ate breakfast.

It was great spending this time with my parents. I thank God every day that he blessed and born me to them.

Holding my hands, we chatted and walked to my truck.

Dad prayed with me and left me with these words of encouragement that will never leave me: *God sends things in peace and tranquility. You will know the answer by having peace and calmness. If you don't allow the answer to come to you, I guarantee you will be stressed, angry, and frustrated. That's not the answer you're looking for. You will be able to feel the presence of peace, reassurance, and comfort. That will let you know when you have those feelings of sensation; you conquered and claimed the victory.*

When I returned home, I sat in the driveway for a few minutes before going inside.

I had watched this house being built from the beginning; the laying of the foundation to the last appliance set in place.

It was beautiful. But now it was built on lies...everything a lie.

I opened the front door and sat my duffle bag on the floor.

Everything still in place, so I went upstairs and checked his closet and drawers... nothing removed.

This jerk is really trying to disturb my inner peace... guess he didn't take me serious when I said be out before I return.

I had to take hold of my life and think about self-preservation. Scrambling through my closet, I took my wedding dress out the garment bag, spread it over the bed, and threw the wedding rings on top.

Just wanted him to think about our wedding vows and his destruction.

I grabbed some more of personal belongings and headed downstairs.

I took one last look and sighed at my new beautifully furnished home.

Grabbing everything, I headed out the front door and threw everything in the back of my truck.

Next, I locked the door, removed my house key, and threw it on the doormat.

As I was driving, my mind was racing. Under the circumstances I had to make a decision to survive and benefit me. But if I stayed and accepted everything, I would lose my self-worth, dignity, and respect. I was not going to throw up my hands and self-destruct... absolutely not. That environment would be too toxic and I had to remove myself as soon as possible.

I pulled over into the drug store to get some hygiene items and snacks.

On my way out the store, I grabbed an apartment guide book. I needed to think and get myself on track and return back to work.

While sitting in my truck, I had to make some adjustments, so I quickly found an apartment. I decided to rent a room at the Extended Stay for three weeks until my new home was ready. Then, I immediately made some appointments, especially with my doctor to get a full STD screen on myself...I n*ever played Russian Roulette with my life and would not start now.*

*W*hen I moved into my apartment, I had to start over from scratch. I made my bed every night on the floor, used plastic dinnerware, and read. Each day got easier with prayer and my family on my side. I slowly decorated and furnished my place.

Needless to say, I was happy and stress-free. I found my peace through intense introspection and later forgiveness.

God lets you see things when put into a situation. I got the victory by prevailing. I had go on with my life. No one was going to live my life but me.

The decision to act was casted upon me. But I asked in the name of Jesus, trust that he will deliver me, and I received his blessing.

Most of all that brought me to this present day was my dad saying, "Do you remember Footprints?"

I smiled and replied to him, "Those one set of footprints I see in the sand is God carrying me."

Dad continued, "God had the answer for you before you knew the answer. Victory is yours, baby, because you prevailed."

I won this battle! My victory!

I have the God-given intestinal fortitude to overcome any obstacle. Sharing this story, any woman can have the victory when she values her self-worth.

God Bless...

NICHOLE PAGE IS a Laboratory Scientist with Duke University Medical Center and North Carolina State Laboratory of Public Health. She earned her Bachelor of Science from Lincoln University in Pennsylvania and still continuing her education. She is also a member of Sigma Gamma Rho Sorority. Nichole loves to travel and has an appreciation for fine wine, art, and history. "House of Lies" is Nichole's first authored short story in Turning Trials into Triumphs. Nichole Page lives in Durham, North Carolina.

THE PERFECT DAUGHTER

We often breathe a sigh of relief after delivering a baby with no outward signs of health issues. We allow ourselves to relax in the knowledge that all is well with our perfect little son or daughter.

However, we are not prepared to discover that there is something not right later on. We allow ourselves that moment of utter shock—that time to fall apart ... but then we have to rise up because there is work to be done, and our children are depending on us.

CHAPTER 1

I say this because I know what I am planning
for you," says the Lord. "I have good plans
for you, not plans to hurt you. I will give
you hope and a good future.

Jeremiah 29:11

All I can remember saying on that cold windy day in November is, "I don't understand..." In a haze, I found myself lying on the floor, struggling to gain clarity from the fuzzy images in my head.

"Who are you and why am I lying on floor?" I asked in confusion.

"Trena, I'm Dr. Mathis. You passed out just as I began telling you about Sasha's condition."

Perplexity whirling around me, I gathered myself as Dr. Mathis' words echoed in my ear. I couldn't help but shift my thoughts to a happier time. I could still see her lips moving although my brain was not allowing my mind to receive the message.

I had reverted back to a sunny day in June, I was thirteen years old and my secret place of refuge was on my grandparent's farm in Creedmoor, North Carolina. The wide open acreage made me feel free—like I could do and be anyone I wanted to be.

This particular day, I was in my favorite pink ruffle dress, sitting by the old oak tree in the middle of the farm taking in the array of blues in the sky, the smell of the budding Gardenia's whisk past my nostril as my head rested on the tree. I busied my thoughts with dreams of one day becoming a teacher, doctor, or maybe even a lawyer. Not once did I dream of becoming a mother—the mother of a child with a physical impairment. It's not something that anyone would predict, but it is in fact, a reality.

Life hadn't always been easy for me, growing up in a dysfunctional household. I was born to a teenage mother who despite hard times, loved me and my siblings as best she knew how, but becoming widowed at twenty-five years old and losing both her brother and father, caused her life to spiral out of control.

She went from men to drugs and it appeared that her children had no place in her life.

How could she do this to us? Did she love us?

Out of my pain, I searched for answers but after a while, it eventually didn't matter to me because I was determined to find someone who would love me. I deserved to be loved—this much I knew. What I didn't know was what lay ahead in the journey of my life.

CHAPTER 2

$\mathcal{M}$y plan to find love didn't go exactly as I had planned.

I was now a senior in high school and the mother of a one-year-old daughter.

A mother.

Not exactly what I'd had in mind, but I didn't run away from my responsibility. I had no idea what I was going to do, but looking at my baby girl—I had no other choice but to get my life together.

Old memories of my young childhood flashed through my mind and I made a decision. I had once dreamed of being a teacher.

I decided it's exactly what I would do--I would go to college and become a teacher. With that goal in mind, I obtained a scholarship to North Carolina Central University where I set out to become somebody with my beautiful daughter by my side. She was my motivation.

I was going to make her proud.

I was determined to be a good mother and a great

student. I had to make this work because my daughter depended on me to provide the best life I could for her.

* * *

ALTHOUGH I WASN'T FOCUSED on having a man in my life—I met someone I thought would be an important part of my life. Things were great between us for a while, however, I should have known it was too good to be true when we moved in together. It was then that I discovered just how toxic we were as a couple.

Just as my life appeared to be back on track, here I was, Trena Gentry, twenty-six years old and expecting my second daughter. Despite everything happening around me, I found myself looking forward to meeting my new bundle of joy and could not wait to hold her in my arms. Once again, I vowed to be the best mother possible.

CHAPTER 3

*O*n Sunday, November 14, 1999, I finally heard the words that every mother longs to hear after laboring to bring a child into the world.

"Congratulations, you have a healthy baby girl…"

I was ecstatic about my beautiful newborn that God had just blessed me with. She was perfect—my gift from above.

I was happy. Maybe even beyond happy. I had two beautiful children whom I loved more than I ever could imagine.

Life couldn't get any better than this.

In the days to come, I soon discovered something was different about my precious gift. Her legs seem to dangle. She did not move as my first child did. Although I knew each baby was different—I felt deep down that something wasn't right. *Why wasn't she moving her legs like most babies?* This couldn't be right. *What's wrong with my Sasha?* I wondered. Not only did I notice her legs seemed to dangle, but there was also an unusual marking on the skin of her lower back.

After several trips to the doctor's office and me being adamant that there was something wrong with Sasha.

The doctors finally diagnosed Sasha with a Tethered

Spinal Cord, which is associated with Spina Bifida. Even though, I didn't have a clue as to what they were talking about; for a moment it felt like my heart had stopping beating.

"Sasha has a what?" was my reply.

Dr. Mathis began to explain that a normal spinal cord floats free inside the spinal canal, but Sasha's spinal cord was fixed to the spinal canal causing weakness and numbness in her lower extremities and would eventually lead to urinary incontinence, scoliosis and back pain. Dr. Mathis was hopeful that having a surgical procedure to "untether" the spinal cord from the spinal tissue would allow Sasha to have a normal life.

* * *

THE DAY OF HER SURGERY, I sat in the waiting room with so many thoughts going through my mind for what seemed like forever. I breathed a sigh of relief when they finally let me see her. However, I was not prepared seeing her with all the tubes coming from what appeared to be her lifeless body after surgery.

Lord, why? I don't understand why you would do this to me.

After being lost in my thoughts, I snapped back to the reality of what the doctor had just told me.

My heart ached with an intense inner pain. I didn't want to believe it. Sasha had added a twinkle to my eyes, a sparkle in my heart, and so much joy to my life! She was the heartbeat of my home. Surely this couldn't be happening. I was so angry.

I feared the unknown but I recognized that I had choices. I was going to do one of two things: forget everything and run or face everything and rise. One thing I knew for sure was that the decision was mine. There wasn't anything else in my control—only the way I would respond. In times of trouble, fear or pain, one has to decide on the proper response. However, we have to be able to move past our emotions.

This was my challenge.

CHAPTER 4

I was beyond furious with God. I felt betrayed and abandoned by the One who promises to always be there. It was the ultimate betrayal and my anger left unrelenting. How could such a loving God be so cruel? I wondered. I couldn't understand why a God who was supposed to love me greatly would not bless me with a healthy baby girl.

Another question entered my troubled thoughts. What had I done to make God so mad that my child had to endure the cruel, harshness, of society?

No answers came which only infuriated me more. It just didn't seem fair. There are so many people who have children that they don't want and those children are born perfect. Was God trying to punish me? This question gnawed at me constantly.

Sitting in Lenox Baker, the hospital where several specialty doctors come together every third Thursday out of the month to see children with some form of Spina Bifida, as I'm waiting for my daughter to be called, another parent said, "I wish my child was doing half of what your child is doing."

Her words stunned me. *What? Wait... ma'am can't you see I'm grieving for my own child? How can you say that...?* While my head was filled with those questions, I politely replied, "Thank you."

Walking back into the examination room, the woman's words played over and over in my head. It was at that moment I realized I needed to stop looking at my daughter's circumstances. I needed to keep my eyes on God and trust that He had my best interests at heart. I thought about the woman who had been in the reception area—she saw what I had not—just how extraordinary my daughter was, despite having a Tethered Spinal Cord. She saw beyond my daughter's condition, recognizing her strength, courage and determination.

So many times, we focus on our issues, concerns, problems, trials, etc. Instead of acknowledging the problem, giving it to God and moving on—we reside permanently in our pain and disappointment. We move in with our pain, taking up residence in the sea of bitterness and pity.

Sasha has always been my special gift from the Lord and I've gained so many teachable moments just in being her mother. She has never seen herself as anything other than a normal little girl—a normal teen—and now a normal young adult.

I always hated when the doctors attempted to treat Sasha as if she was some textbook case.

They couldn't have been more wrong.

I made it clear that she *would* walk; she was not going to struggle in her learning—she would defy the odds. It was my declaration, my decree and my faith that God would be with Sasha every step of the way.

My daughter continues to defy the odds and seems to welcome the challenge of someone telling her what she can't do.

Yeah right… is her attitude. Bring it on.

* * *

EVEN THOUGH I was broken and devastated; today, I shout victory as I see my beautiful daughter take, one day at a time, one step at a time, blossoming into the young lady God has created her to be. Even though she walks with forearm crutches they do not define her.

Today, I realize that although she came through my birth canal, she is truly a blessing from God. He molded her especially for me with a purpose in mind. I understand she is destined to succeed and change the world.

Three surgeries, four MRIs, multiple tests, and countless hours of physical therapy, but Sasha is thriving, excelling, and living life to the fullest. I know longer feel sorry for myself or her. She is beating the odds… Top of her class, driving, in show choir have a great group of friends… preparing for college—truly enjoying her teenage years. My daughter is an honor student, a member of the National Honor Society, she plays the piano; she played baseball and soccer. She's a fabulous singer and enjoys show choir. In her spare time, she volunteers to give back to the community.

CHAPTER 5

*W*e all want this perfect little bundle of joy, but what is perfect?

Perfection is born out of challenges, finding courage, being victorious, and an overcomer. You can't strive to move on if you hold on to a victim mentality.

I taught my daughter that there were no limitations for her. I made sure she understood her power, her capabilities, and most important—her worth. Sasha knows that she is a special gift from God—my perfect little bundle of joy.

This disease was supposed to destroy not only my daughter, but me as well. However, God said no. Instead it made us stronger. We may not understand God's plan at the time, but if we hold onto our faith and trust Him with our entire being —He will always reveal his plan for our lives. Proverbs 3:5 tells us, "Trust in the Lord with all thine heart and lean not unto thine own understanding. This is a scripture I live by— it is my mantra.

Sasha is my gift, my blessing from above and I'm so honored to be her mother. I can't imagine my life without her.

In addition to being blessed with the perfect daughter, I recognized how futile it can be to try to fit in when you were created to be set apart. I didn't know my own strength until I was put to the test. Life takes us through storms and trials to build our character.

When I was younger, I dreamed often of happily ever after. I can truly shout from the rooftops that my dream has come true.

CHAPTER 6

*I*n this chapter, I want to share some of the scriptures that encouraged me during this journey. These are words to live by and I urge you to meditate on them. In order to move from trials to triumphs, you have to know the Word of God.

Isaiah 55:8-9 "My thoughts," says the Lord, "are not like yours, and my ways are different from yours. As high as the heavens are above the earth, so high are my ways and thoughts above yours.

1 Peter 5:7 casting all your care upon Him, for He cares for you.

Romans 8:28 We know that God makes all things work together for the good of those who love Him and are chosen to be a part of His plan.

Psalm 139:13-16 You alone created my inner being. You knitted me together inside my mother. I will give thanks to you because I have been so amazingly and miraculously made. Your works are miraculous, and my soul is fully aware of this. My bones were not hidden from you when I was being made in secret, when I was being skillfully woven in an underground workshop. Your eyes saw me when I was still an unborn child. Every day of my life was recorded in your book before one of them had taken place.

Psalm 56: 8 You keep track of all my sorrows. You have collected all my tears in your bottle. You have recorded each one in your book.

It is important that you remember that what you are confessing is manifesting, so speak life over your situations and dare to believe. You see, I had to trust God and lean not to my own understanding for God is the great I AM—the Great Physician. I couldn't just buy into what the doctors were saying initially, but when I pushed my emotions aside, I realized that God is and has always been the Master Physician.

I want to encourage you to meet every challenge as an opportunity for God to show Himself strong in your life. Always remember that God hands His toughest battles to His greatest fighters. When faced with your greatest trials, rise up and know that whatsoever you declare in Jesus Name, it shall be done. You just have to recognize that God's time is not our time, yet He is always on time. Just trust and have faith in Him.

TRACEY BURWELL-DESHAZO, *wife and mother of two, releases her first story about her youngest daughter. "The Perfect Daughter" showcases a difficult time in DeShazo's life as she had to raise a daughter with a physical limitation. DeShazo used this experience to mentor the youth at church and inspire them to live in God's blessings. She works in the administrative side of Emergency Medical Services, but plans to open up a center for teenage moms in the future. You can contact Tracey at: traceydeshazowrites@gmail.com.*

DISCUSSION GUIDE

1. What is the proper response when going through trials? How do we retain our joy in the midst of storms that have come to wreck our lives?
2. What specific themes were emphasized throughout the book?
3. Can you relate to any of the situations in the book? To what extent do the people in the book remind you of yourself or someone you know?
4. Can you point to a particular passage that struck you personally? Did you learn something new or broaden your perspective? Please elaborate.
5. If you had to describe this book in one word— what would it be?
6. Why does God allow trials in our lives?
7. The contributors in this anthology believe that their stories will help others. How has the sharing of their testimonies helped you?
8. What did you like best about this anthology? What did you like least?

9. Was there anything surprising about any of the stories? What was it and why?
10. After reading this book, are you ready to turn your trials into triumphs?

Made in the USA
Columbia, SC
10 July 2020

12720625R00098